THE DEAD SEA COMMUNITY

THE DEAD SEA COMMUNITY

Its Origin and Teachings

BY KURT SCHUBERT

*Professor of Jewish Religion and Culture
in the University of Vienna*

TRANSLATED BY JOHN W. DOBERSTEIN

HARPER & BROTHERS · PUBLISHERS
NEW YORK

PREFACE

IN response to requests from various quarters, I decided to develop into a small book the lectures on the texts of Khirbet Qumrân which I delivered in the summer of 1957 in the philosophical faculty of Arts and Sciences in the University of Vienna for members of all faculties, and which I also delivered for the Zionistic Federation in Austria in the winter semester of 1957–8. I have summed up in this present volume, as I did in the lectures, the results of my research on these texts up to this time, a labour which has now covered almost ten years. I desired to retain the original structure of the lectures in the printed form, in order that I might not be tempted to enter into discussion of technical details and thus make the book unintelligible to a broader circle of readers. Therefore, as was done in the lectures, in which annotations must also be avoided, I have incorporated quotations and other absolutely necessary references into the text and dispensed with footnotes. I have also avoided any extensive discussion with specialists, since it is impossible to do this in any satisfactory way in terms which would be intelligible to everybody, and besides, this would have overburdened the book. For most of the problems dealt with in this book I have already presented my scientific evidence in the academic journals. Readers who are interested in my arguments and discussion with the scholars will find in Appendix 3 a list of my published works on the Qumrân texts. In order not to overload the general survey of the literature, I have in principle omitted the inclusion of periodical articles, the number of which already runs into thousands. Therefore only *books* on the new discoveries are included in Appendix 1 and only text editions in *book* form are included in Appendix 2.

The present volume, like the lectures, was designed from the beginning to be different from most of the books on the Dead Sea discoveries hitherto published. Problems such as, for example, the general dating of the scrolls in the period between the Old and the New Testaments, on which there is almost complete agreement, are therefore not discussed here again but simply briefly mentioned. Instead, however, it seemed to me to be important to point out that the sect cannot have come out of the blue at the beginning of the second century before Christ, but that many of its ideas and teachings have Old Testament antecedents. My chief interest, however, lay in setting out the teachings of the Qumrân community and their relationships to the New Testament and to Pharisaic-Talmudic-Rabbinic Judaism.

The new discoveries are unquestionably of the utmost importance for the history of Jewish religion in the period from about 200 B.C. to A.D. 100; they open up hitherto undreamed-of perspectives, and yet they ought not to be over-rated. It is certain that the Dead Sea community is a group which is paradigmatic of the Messianic movement of the Judaism of that time. But how many such groups were there? It is true that we can assert with considerable certainty that the books discovered in the caves near Qumrân and not contained in our Hebrew Bible were disseminated in the Qumrân community and in all probability were held in high regard there, but we do not know whether they were read exclusively in this community or where else they may have been read. The only thing we can assert with approximate certainty is that some— but by no means all—of these books were rejected by Pharisaic and Sadducaic Judaism. Despite all these reservations, however the texts discovered in the caves at the Dead Sea constitute the best source we have so far for the religious and historical understanding of the milieu of the New Testament. Therein also lies their great significance, which not without reason made them a "sensation".

Vienna   KURT SCHUBERT

NOTE

The Biblical quotations throughout are in the text of the Revised Standard Version.

CONTENTS

I

THE TEXTS

IN order to avoid confusion the following terms are used: those books which are contained in the Hebrew Bible, the so-called Masoretic texts, are referred to as biblical or Old Testament books; those books which do not appear in the Hebrew canon but only in the Greek canon of the Septuagint are termed deuterocanonical books; but those books which appear in neither of these canons are included under the general title of "pseudepigrapha".

I. THE BIBLICAL TEXTS OF THE HEBREW CANON

Smaller or larger fragments of almost all the biblical texts were found in the caves. Most of these texts are written in the square script still used in printing; several, however, are written in the older Phoenician script.

ISAIAH SCROLL "A" (published by Millar Burrows): This scroll consists of seventeen pieces of sheepskin sewn together with thread and is divided into fifty-four columns. It is 24 ft. long and 10 ins. in height. The Isaiah "A" scroll provides the complete text of the prophet Isaiah and proves that the Masoretic text was based on good traditions. Nevertheless, the scroll provides a series of variants which are of interest to the specialist but not to the general reader. As in several other texts, the so-called *scriptio plena* frequently occurs as a reading aid for the vocalization of the vowels. As in other scrolls, a number of endings and full vowels are retained which in Masoretic Hebrew disappeared altogether or became unaccented vowels.

ISAIAH SCROLL "B" (published by E. L. Sukenik): In contrast to Isaiah Scroll "A" this scroll is not in a good state of preservation. It is written on sheepskin and, like Scroll "A", consists of a number of pieces sewn together. However, only one of these parchments, the last but one, containing chapters 52–61, is preserved in its entirety. But even here more than a third is missing at the margin. A fairly coherent text begins with chapter 41 and runs through to the end of the scroll. But fragments of the earlier chapters have also been preserved, the first fragment being from chapter 10. Thus it is by pure accident that this scroll contains precisely these portions of Deutero- and Trito-Isaiah, for, as the fragments of chapter 10–39 show, the older portions were also a part of this scroll. Generally speaking, it too demonstrates the good transmission of the texts by the Masoretes and its orthography is also closer to the Masoretic text than that of Scroll "A" in that it has fewer reading aids than the latter. The two Isaiah scrolls show that at the time they were copied there were two orthographies in use, one probably ancient, with fewer reading aids, which the Masoretes made their own, and the other with more reading aids, which probably served for "domestic use".

2. DEUTEROCANONICAL WRITINGS

In Cave II, were found two fragments of the Book of Ecclesiasticus and in Cave IV three fragments of the Book of Tobit, of which one is in Hebrew on leather and two in Aramaic, one on leather and one on papyrus (not yet published).

3. PSEUDEPIGRAPHA

a) Sectarian Writings

(*Pseudepigrapha hitherto unknown through secondary translations*)

i. From Cave I

HABAKKUK COMMENTARY (published by Millar Burrows):
This scroll consists of two pieces of leather sewn together,
comprising a total of thirteen columns. Excluding one
fragment which contains the left side of column one and
the right side of column two, it is 4 feet 11 inches long. If
we assume that columns one and two had an average
length comparable to the length of the other columns, the
scroll must originally have been approximately 5 feet
3 inches in length. At present it has a maximum height of
$5\frac{1}{2}$ inches, though the bottom of each column is missing.
The text of columns three to thirteen, apart from the lost
lower margin, is relatively well preserved, though the first
two columns show severe damage. The scroll presents
a commentary on the first two chapters of the Book of
Habakkuk. The author attempts to reinterpret the events
described by the prophet in a contemporary way, so as to
make them point to the circumstances of his own life. In
doing so he employs pseudonyms exclusively, giving no
proper names, either of persons or of groups. On the
author's side stands the "Teacher of Righteousness" with
his followers, whose life is a "ministry of truth". The
Teacher of Righteousness is viewed as the prophet of the
last days, to whom has been revealed even that which
remained hidden from the prophets in their preaching.
The author demands faith in the message and the absolute prophetic dignity of the Teacher of Righteousness
from those who desire to belong to the elect community
of the "New Covenant". Ranged against the Teacher of

Righteousness are at least two groups: a) the "Man of Lies" with the "men of violence" and the "apostates"; b) the "Wicked Priest" and his group. As a possible third group, which, however, must once have been close to the followers of the Teacher of Righteousness, a "house of Absolom" is mentioned. However, the two large groups hostile to the community were themselves involved in bitter quarrels. Thus in 8, 11 we read that the Wicked Priest "robbed and pillaged the wealth of the men of violence who had rebelled against God." The Wicked Priest may possibly be understood to refer to King Alexander Jannaeus (103–76 B.C.) and the men of violence and apostates are very probably the Pharisees (the term "apostates" may also have included other, non-Pharisaic groups), while the group of the Teacher of Righteousness, who himself cannot be convincingly identified with an historical person, may have belonged to the wider association of Essene communities.

Also in Cave I there were found fragmentary commentaries on *Micah*, *Zephaniah*, and the *Psalms* (published by Barthélemy and Milik). In the Micah commentary the Teacher of Righteousness and the Preacher of Lies are mentioned as in the Habakkuk commentary.

WAR SCROLL (published by E. L. Sukenik, text and commentary by Yigael Yadin): The War Scroll consists of five fragments stitched together, the fifth fragment consisting of no more than a small remainder. As in the Habakkuk commentary and the Isaiah Scroll "B", the lower portion of the text is also missing here. The scroll is 9 feet 5 inches long and about 6⅓ inches high, and contains nineteen columns of writing. The contents of the scroll indicate that the community from which it originated was awaiting an eschatological war of the "sons of light" against the "sons of darkness". Only the community itself belongs to the sons of light, whereas all others are numbered among the "worthless heathen" (i.e., the heathen who have no relevance to the history of salvation) or to the "violators of the covenant". The elect members of the community are living at the time in the desert, which is felt to be a place of salvation where the Messianic redemption would begin to reveal itself (cf. Isa. 4:3). During an eschatological period of forty years the enemies of God will be fought and conquered one after another by the elect members of the community, who will be accompanied by the angels in the final battle, and thus the rule of God will be extended over the whole world. During the sabbatical years there is to be no fighting, because these years are to be devoted to rest and the worship of God. In contrast to the Pharisees and Sadducees this community counted the years according to a solar calendar and not according to a lunar calendar. The eschatological battle is described down to the last detail. Three times the sons of light will conquer by virtue of their own strength and three times the sons of darkness will conquer, but in the seventh engagement the "strong hand of God" will bring the decisive victory.

HYMN SCROLL (published by E. L. Sukenik, commentary and text by Jacob Licht): The scroll is preserved in two separate parts. The first part consists of three leaves of leather comprising a total of twelve columns. The second part consists of about seventy larger and smaller fragments, from which it is possible to reconstruct six further complete columns and a number of incomplete columns. It runs to 12⅔ inches in height. This scroll presents the theology of the community in prayer form and lays great emphasis upon the all-embracing providence of God and the election of the individual. Some scholars have conjectured that their author was the Teacher of Righteousness.

THE MANUAL OF DISCIPLINE (published by Millar Burrows): The Manual of Discipline consists of five strips of leather which present a continuous text of eleven columns which are slightly damaged only at the bottom edge. The beginning of the first column is also not quite complete. In its present state this scroll is a little over 5 feet 11 inches long and about $9\frac{1}{2}$ inches high. With regard to content, the Manual of Discipline is divided into four sections, an introduction, a Gnostic-sounding section of teachings, the actual statutes, and a concluding hymn. The regulations in the statutory section as well as many elements in the introduction are closely related to the accounts given by Flavius Josephus and Philo of Alexandria concerning Essenism. In the main it may be concluded from these sections that these writings belong to the wider circle of Essene communities. The Gnostic-sounding didactic section exhibits close affiliations with Stoic-Platonic popular philosophy. Likewise it is possible that the formation of the Light-Darkness doctrine presented here is not entirely uninfluenced by Iranian conceptions. The opposing forces of light and darkness are described, headed by their own companies of angels. Light and darkness are both created by God and yet "at the fixed time of his visitation" he will destroy darkness forever. In the closing hymn, as in the above-mentioned Hymn Scroll, the question of the relation of the decisions of the human will to divine providence is raised.

THE BOOK OF RULES (published by Barthélemy and Milik): The Book of Rules consists of two relatively well-preserved columns as well as a series of fragments which contain a number of hymns of praise. In the opinion of the editor, the above-mentioned Manual of Discipline and this Book of Rules were originally a single scroll, in which case the Book of Rules would be considered a continuation of the Manual of Discipline. However this may be, the Book of Rules deals with different data and starts from different presuppositions from those of the Manual of Discipline. Whereas the Manual of Discipline deals with a monastic community, the precepts of the Book of Rules are addressed to the married members of the community. In the second column reference is also made to what is very probably a ritual meal in which bread and wine play an essential part. This banquet, which is to take place in the last days in the messianic era is attended by two Messiahs, a high-priestly Messiah and a lay Messiah from the non-priestly ranks of the people of Israel. The latter, as comparison with other texts indicates, is quite certainly to be identified with the new David-Messiah. The priestly Messiah is hierarchically superior to the lay Messiah; he stands at the head of the priests and the lay Messiah at the head of the officers. The songs of praise, which are preserved only in fragments, are intended first for the members of the community in general, then for the (probably messianic) high priest, then for the other priests, and finally for the Davidic-messianic princes of the community (cf. Ezek. 37:25).

THE GENESIS APOCRYPHON (published by Avigad and Yadin) consists of four leather pieces of unequal length sewn together. Their height is about 12 inches and the length of the scroll, of which the beginning and the end are missing, is 9 feet 3 inches. Only columns twenty to twenty-two are preserved in good legible condition and several other columns are tolerably readable. This scroll

7

could not be unrolled for a long time. It was originally the property of the Syrian Archbiship Athanasius Samuel and was to have been published by the American School of Oriental Research, which, however, did not risk opening the scroll. Therefore it was not unrolled and published until 1956, after it had been purchased by the Hebrew University together with the other scrolls in the possession of the Syrian Archbishop. Unlike the other texts mentioned so far, this scroll is written in Aramaic. It contains portions of a Lamech, Noah, and Abraham tradition, which is related to the corresponding sections in the Book of Jubilees and the Ethiopic Book of Enoch.

ii. From the Other Caves

In Cave IV eleven as yet unpublished manuscripts of the Manual of Discipline were discovered, two of them on papyrus. Some of them are said to contain variants of the copy of the Manual of Discipline discovered in Cave I. Also in Cave IV there were discovered four as yet unpublished copies of the War Scroll, which are said to contain variants of this document. Six copies of the Hymn Scroll, still unpublished, one of them on papyrus, were also found in Cave IV. In Cave III the excavators discovered two copper scrolls, which though they were unrolled in 1956, have not yet been published. They are said to contain directions concerning buried treasures, some of these treasures said to be hidden under the grave of the priest Zadok, the progenitor of the Zadokite priests. (Several fragments of an older version of the War Scroll were published by Claus-Hunno Hunzinger, *Zeitschrift für die alttestamentliche Wissenschaft* (69 [1957], pp. 131–51.)

In Cave IV an esoteric work was also discovered in which the words are written from right to left, as is normal in Hebrew, but the individual letters are written from left to right. It also contains a mixture of Phoenician, Hebrew, Greek, and secret letters. Although this work has not yet been published, these extraordinary circumstances permit us to conclude that it must contain secret teachings of the community.

Another as yet unpublished text from Cave IV contains a heavenly liturgy which is supposed to be related to the so-called Merkava literature. This document, should it prove to bear a close relationship to the later rabbinical-Gnostic Merkava texts, would show that the beginnings of Jewish gnosticism were elements in the teaching of this community.

In Cave IV were also found commentaries on the Books of Isaiah, Hosea, Nahum, and Psalms. The commentaries on Psalm 37 and the prophet Nahum have already been published (J. M. Allegro, *Palestine Exploration Quarterly* 86 [1954], pp. 69–75; *Journal of Biblical Literature* 75 [1956], pp. 89–95). In the commentary on Psalm 37 the "Teacher of Righteousness" is mentioned as in the commentary on Habakkuk from Cave I, and in the commentary on the prophet Nahum the names of historical persons appear for the first time in these texts. These are Demetrius, king of the Greeks, apparently the Seleucid Demetrius III (summoned by the Pharisees in 88 B.C. to aid them against Alexander Jannaeus) and Antiochus, who may be either Antiochus III (223–187 B.C.) or Antiochus IV (175–164 B.C.).

A series of Messianic texts was also found in Cave IV. These have been published at least in part (J. M. Allegro, *Journal of Biblical Literature* 75 [1956,] pp. 174–187). They are:

Patriarchal Blessings: Here the Messiah of the house of

David is called the Messiah of righteousness, scion of David.

Messianic Florilegium: Here in connection with the prophecy of Nathan concerning David (II Sam. 7:11–14) there is a description of the Davidic Messiah who will appear in the last days together with the "Teacher of the Torah". It is very probable that the pseudonym "Teacher of the Torah", which also occurs in the Damascus document, refers to the priestly Messiah.

Messianic Testimonies: Here the following biblical passages follow one another: Deut. 5:28–9 (with reference to Moses); Deut. 18:18–19 (a prophetic Moses); Num. 24:15–17 (oracle of Balaam); Deut. 33:8–11 (Moses' blessing upon Levi); Josh. 6:26 (curse upon the rebuilder of Jericho). The Messianic Testimonies therefore deal with the same doctrine of the Messiah which is presupposed in the Manual of Discipline 9:11, "until the coming of the Prophet and the Messiahs of Aaron and Israel". First, reference is made to the new prophet like Moses, then follow the two Messiahs of Aaron and Israel symbolized in the oracle of Balaam, and finally the priestly head of the whole community is emphasized by means of Moses' blessing upon Levi.

In the Commentary on Isaiah 11:1–4 the Davidic Messiah, who will rule over all nations and judge them with the sword, is again described. Isa. 11:3 is here interpreted as meaning that the Davidic Messiah will judge, not according to his own discretion, but in accordance with the instruction of the priests.

*b) Pseudepigrapha already known through
Secondary Translations or Medieval Hebrew Transcripts*

The Damascus Document (published by Salomon Schechter, *Documents of Jewish Sectaries*, vol. i; *Fragments of a Zadokite Work*, Cambridge, 1910; Leonhard Rost, *Die Damaskus-schrift*, Berlin, 1933 (in Lietzmann's Kleine Texte); Chaim Rabin, *The Zadokite Documents*, Oxford, 1954): In Cave VI a fragment of the Damascus Document was found and in Cave IV seven fragmentary manuscripts, one of them on papyrus, were discovered. The Damascus Document was already known from medieval transcripts which were discovered at the turn of the century in the Genizah of the Karaite synagogue in Old Cairo. In content it is very similar to the Habakkuk Commentary as well as the Manual of Discipline and in addition presents a brief summary of the history of the community. The experts do not agree on the question whether the migration to Damascus described in this text actually took place or whether this too is merely to be construed symbolically. Here again we encounter the "Teacher of Righteousness", the "Preacher of Lies", and the idea of the "New Covenant". However, at least in part, a social structure is presupposed which is different from that of the Manual of Discipline.

In Cave I six small Hebrew fragments of the Book of Jubilees were found, in Cave II two Hebrew fragment of the same book, and in Cave IV five Hebrew fragments, one of them on papyrus. These fragments of the Book of Jubilees prove that the Latin and Ethiopian translations provide relatively good versions of the original text.

In Cave IV ten fragmentary Aramaic manuscripts of the Book of Enoch were found, which are in part fuller than the Ethiopic Enoch. In all ten manuscripts, the second part or so-called Similitudes, chapters 37–71, in other words precisely those passages which deal with the Son of Man-Messiah, are missing. The absence of the Son of Man-Messiah concept in the Essene texts of Khirbet

Qumrân may therefore not be accidental. In Cave I as well as Cave IV Aramaic fragments of the Testament of Levi were also found. These finds prove that the pseud-epigrapha mentioned belong both religiously and historically to the sphere of the above-mentioned sectarian writings and thus have their origins among the Essenic communities. Recently portions of the Testament of Naphtali in Hebrew have also been identified among the fragments of texts available to the scholars. Both the Testament of Levi and the Testament of Naphtali belong to the larger corpus of the Testaments of the Twelve Patriarchs, which was given its final textual form by a (Jewish)-Christian editor.

(In this account we have included only those texts which are extant in several fragments, or those which are not too small to be used. Texts which consist of very small fragments, and about which therefore nothing substantial can be said, have been omitted.)

II

THE QUESTION OF THE CANON

THE fact that biblical as well as extra-biblical texts were found in the caves of Qumrân presents us with the question whether all of these texts or only a part of them were viewed by the religious community in whose circle they were read as holy and divinely inspired scriptures. A final and in every respect satisfactory answer is hardly possible. On the one hand it is certain that a community which was preparing for the immediately imminent last days did not concern itself with any "profane" literature. On the other hand it is very probable that not all texts were of equal sanctity for the members of the sect. If, for example, the eleven still unpublished fragments of the Manual of Discipline from Cave IV contain a number of variants from the copy found in Cave I, as it is said to do, then it is very probable that here we are dealing with a document which was not considered to be literally inspired, but simply contained the rules of the community which in the course of time underwent modifications suited to the circumstances. Thus texts which contain essentially different readings in several manuscripts may be considered as having subordinate sanctity for the community. Nevertheless, the canon of the Essene community near the Dead Sea may have been more extensive than the later Masoretic canon. Besides the customary books of the Hebrew Bible,

those writings which contain such concrete sectarian doctrines of this community as are recognized in other writings
as incontestably prerequisite may have been accepted as
canonical. Thus, the Book of Jubilees, for example, may
have been counted as canonical, because in chapter
6:22–38, a calendar of three hundred and sixty-four days,
i.e. fifty-two weeks, is mentioned as being registered by
God's will upon the heavenly tables. Thus the point here
is that this is a solar calendar, whereas the Pharisees and
Sadducees reckoned according to a lunar calendar. This
calendar of the Book of Jubilees is assumed in the War
Scroll and thus the view of the Book of Jubilees that the
solar calendar is written on the heavenly tables may have
been considered by the community to be a canonical doctrine. Thus other writings besides the usual books of the
Old Testament may have been regarded as inspired by
the community, though at this date it is still impossible to
make any more precise statements with regard to the
exact number of these writings in a canon.

Certain apocalyptic revelations, such as, for example,
the pronouncements of the Teacher of Righteousness
concerning the last days, may well have been considered
canonical, since the Teacher of Righteousness is regarded
by the author of the Habakkuk Commentary 7:4–5 as an
inspired prophet, "to whom God made known all the
mysteries of the words of his servants the prophets".
Moreover, it is also stated in the Habakkuk Commentary
8:1–2 that those who believe in the Teacher of Righteousness will be rescued from the judgment, which means in
the mind of the author of the Habakkuk Commentary
that only those will be justified who accept the concrete
eschatological proclamation of the Teacher as the word of
God.

In the closing decades of the second century before Christ a conservative, bourgeois party, originally allied with the priestly-revisionist group from which the Qumrân texts originated, developed into the party of Pharisaism. The most important element in the controversy between the newly-developed Pharisaism and the priestly radicalists of Qumrân was that of the teaching concerning the last things. The pharisees refused to recognize the various apocalyptic enunciations as inspired. We have a Tanaitic saying which expresses this view: "After Haggai, Zachariah, and Malachi, the last prophets, died, the Holy Spirit disappeared from Israel" (Tosephta Sotah XIII,2; Yoma 9b; Sotah 48b; Sanhedrin 11a). With this dictum Pharisaism circumscribed the prophetic books with the canon of the minor prophets and rejected all the pseudepigraphical writings which were published with the claim of being prophetically inspired. The expanded canon of the people of Khirbet Qumrân thus brought about the delimitation of the more circumscribed canon of our Hebrew Bible.

III

THE AGE OF THE TEXTS

THE question of the age of the manuscripts themselves is not directly bound up with the question of the age of the texts. Some of the manuscripts may be considerably more recent than the texts, but of course the texts cannot be more recent than the manuscripts. Thus, for example, the biblical texts among the Qumrân scrolls are essentially older than their manuscripts, whereas the sectarian writings, in part at least, cannot be (much) older than their manuscripts. Naturally, here again there is the possibility that the content of the texts may be a hundred to a hundred and fifty years older than the manuscripts, but generally speaking the question of the internal dating of the individual scrolls is less important than their proper chronological classification in the intertestamental period. For the determination of the age of the texts we have at our disposal the following criteria:

a) The linen in which the scrolls found by the Bedouins in 1947 were wrapped was tested by the so-called radiocarbon process and this showed that the linen was produced in the year A.D. 33 plus or minus two hundred years, thus in the period from 168 B.C. to A.D. 233. This refutes from the very outset those theories which designate the texts as medieval forgeries.

b) In the caves a type of ceramic jar was found which is similar to what was discovered within the monastery

16

building at Qumrân. The discovery of a scriptorium and inkwells in the monastery also establishes the connection between this monastic colony and the texts discovered in the caves. Thus the archaeological findings from the excavation of the monastery ruins establish a conclusive chronological determination of the time when the texts were hidden in the caves. Archaeological arguments, which will be dealt with further in our description of the excavations at Qumrân, show with certainty that this monastery was destroyed in the year A.D. 68. Thus the year A.D. 68 is also the *terminus ante quem* for the writing of the texts.

c) Paleographical arguments: Until recently the only material for comparison available was the so-called *Nash papyrus*, which contains the Ten Commandments and the beginning of the Shema, but this itself was dated in the period from the second century before Christ to the second century after Christ. However, in the course of the excavations in Wadi Murabba'at, about ten or eleven miles south of Qumrân, which took place between January 21 and March 3, 1952, texts were found from the time of Bar Kokhba (A.D. 132–5), which are thus clearly dated. The texts present a form of script which is later than that of the Qumrân texts. Thus the paleographical argument points in the same direction as the archaeological.

d) Examination of the content of some of the texts indicates that they describe a time before the year 80 B.C., when the Teacher of Righteousness may have been a contemporary of Alexander Jannaeus (103–76 B.C.). Several scholars (Stauffer and Rowley) date the Teacher of Righteousness as far back as the time of the religious persecutions under Antiochus IV (175–164 B.C.), but this estimate may well be too early.

IV

THE STORY OF THE DISCOVERIES

In the spring of 1947 Bedouins of the tribe of Ta'amireh accidentally discovered Cave I and brought to light the following texts: Isaiah Scroll "A", Isaiah Scroll "B", the Habakkuk Commentary, the Manual of Discipline, the War Scroll, the Hymn Scroll, and the Genesis Apocryphon. Only a small part of the texts, all of which are now in the possession of the Hebrew University in Jerusalem, came originally into its custody. The greater portion was secured by the abbot of the Syrian Orthodox Convent of St. Mark in the Old City of Jerusalem, Mar Athanasius Yeshue Samuel, who released his texts (Isaiah Scroll "A", the Habakkuk Commentary, the Manual of Discipline and the Genesis Apocryphon) to the American School of Oriental Research for publication. The American School published the first three of these texts in exemplary editions in the year 1950–51, and yet the Americans did not dare to unroll the exceedingly fragile scroll of the Genesis Apocryphon. This scroll was unrolled and published in part after all the texts in the possession of the Syrian archbishop had been purchased by the Hebrew University, in the year 1956 in Jerusalem.

Originally the Bedouins kept secret the exact location of the caves, but the Belgian Captain Philippe Lippens of the staff of the United Nations in Palestine succeeded with the support of the Department of Antiquities of the government of Jordan and the Arab Legion in discovering the caves at the end of January 1949. From February 15 to March 5, 1949, excavations were carried out in the cave which prove the absolute genuineness of the Bedouin finds. From potsherds found in the cave it was possible to put together a jar which conformed exactly to the form of a jar which the Bedouins had sold to Professor Sukenik of the Hebrew University. Also found in the cave were fragments of text which fill in the gaps in the manuscripts purchased from the Bedouins. A further series of manuscripts, probably the most important of which was the so-called Book of Rules with the appended songs of praise, was also discovered in the cave.

In the year 1951 the scholars of the École Biblique Dominicaine in the Old City of Jerusalem and the Department of Antiquities of the Hashemite Kingdom of Jordan, which had also carried out the archaeological investigation of the first cave, embarked upon the excavation of monastery ruins of Khirbet Qumrân which is closely related to the cave discoveries. However, even while this excavation was going on the archaeologists were set off on another tack when Bedouins from a region about nine miles south of Qumrân offered fresh texts for sale. Thus from January 21 to March 3, 1952, four caves were investigated in Wadi Murabba'at. The most important find in these caves may turn out to be a letter of Bar Kokhba bearing his own signature. The finds in Wadi Murabba'at have no actual connection with the discoveries at Qumrân.

In the spring of 1952 the Ta'amireh Bediouns discovered the so-called Cave II of Qumrân. From March 10 to 29, 1952, the archaeologists systematically excavated the entire area of Qumrân and on March 14, 1952, discovered the so-called Cave III of Qumrân in which the two copper scrolls were found.

In the summer of 1952 a number of Syrian, Greek, and Arabic texts, which have no connection either with Qumrân or the finds in Wadi Murabba'at, were discovered in the area of Khirbet Mird. Nabatean papyri from another place of origin in the more remote vicinity were also offered for sale. Since these finds do not properly concern us here, we shall not discuss them in detail.

At the beginning of September, 1952, the same Ta'amireh Bedouins discovered the so-called Cave IV of Qumrân and on September 13, 1952, fragments from the so-called Cave VI were offered for sale. From September 22 to 29, 1952, excavations were carried on in Cave IV which proved to be the richest of all the caves found so far. The so-called Cave V of Qumrân was discovered and excavated in the period September 22–24, 1952, and Cave VI was identified on September 27. During the fourth excavation of the monastery ruins of Qumrân, which extended from February 2 to April 6, 1955, Caves VII–X were discovered and just before the fifth excavation, in February 1956, Cave XI was found.

V

THE EXCAVATIONS IN THE MONASTERY RUINS OF KHIRBET QUMRÂN

THE excavations took place on the following dates:

    i. November 24 to December 12, 1951
    ii. April 9 to 24, 1953
    iii. February 13 to April 14, 1954
    iv. February 2 to April 6, 1955
    v. February 18 to March 28, 1956

As long ago as the middle of the last century the ruins at Khirbet Qumrân commanded the attention of archaeologists, though they identified them with a Roman citadel or even with fallen Gomorrah. Because of the finds in the caves, Khirbet Qumrân has, since 1949, come to occupy the foreground of attention. Even on the occasion of the investigation of the first cave in the spring of 1949 there was some superficial digging done on the site of the ruins. Although these test diggings established no connection with the caves, systematic excavation was carried out from 1951 onwards and it was this which proved the existence of such a connection with complete certainty.

The first excavation resulted in the discovery of a main building measuring $98\frac{1}{3}$ by $121\frac{1}{3}$ feet, and a number of coins in Level II. It was during this excavation that the great main cemetery with about a thousand graves to the east of the ruins was discovered, having been recognized by a paving of flint stones. The graves, in which no objects or ornaments were found, are all arranged in a north-south direction so that the head lay toward the south.

In the year 1953 it was possible to establish the fact that the monastery ruins underwent several periods of building and that it was not a dwelling house but rather a "community house" with the appropriate industrial buildings necessary to the community. The inhabitants themselves were probably lodged overnight either in tents nearby or even in the caves. The scriptorium, which had fallen from the upper story, and two inkwells, were also discovered. It was probably in this scriptorium that a large part of the discovered texts were written.

In the year 1954 the area south of the main building was excavated, including an assembly hall. Immediately adjoining it on the south a storage room was discovered, containing 1,080 cups, plates, bowls, and platters, but no cooking utensils, in other words, the tableware of the community. On the plastered floor at the west end of the assembly hall, which also served as a refectory, the place of the presiding officer is visible, marked out by a circle paved with flagstones. The assembly hall was 72 feet 2 inches long and 14 feet 9 inches wide.

During the excavation of 1955 the west half of the area was cleared and an industrial building was discovered, separated from the main building. North of it was still another courtyard and a bath.

In 1956 the rest of the area was cleared, the cemeteries were investigated, and the excavation at 'Ain Feshka a dependency of the monastery situated nearly 2 miles south of Khirbet Qumrân, was begun.

The industrial rooms of the monastery included a kitchen, stables, storerooms, and a potter's workshop with two potter's kilns. But more interesting than these finds are those which throw light upon the peculiar characteristics of the dwellers in these monastery ruins. A specially built water-supply system was discovered. The aqueduct itself fed a series of cisterns, all but two of which have staircases which occupy at least half of their area. It is possible that these cisterns served as baths, and yet similar cisterns have been discovered near Jerusalem without any evidence of their being used for ritual purposes. However, it has been established that two small and well-cared-for basins in the structure of Khirbet Qurmân were used for bathing purposes. One large cistern with no steps definitely served as a reservoir. Thus it is demonstrated that the community was especially concerned with cleanliness and that ritual baths were also a part of their regime. The assembly hall mentioned above, with its specially appointed place for the presiding officer and the storage room for dishes located to the south of it show that meals were taken communally and that one of the participants presided. The Manual of Discipline and the Book of Rules indicate that this president was a priest and that bread and wine, which were blessed by him, also played an especial part in the meal.

In many unroofed places deposits of animal bones stuffed into clay vessels were found; the bones, which were not connected, were clearly gathered together after the flesh had been removed. From the bones themselves it is possible to determine that the animals were those permitted by Jewish ritual and that they were either cooked or roasted. Thus at the communal meals, upon which the blessing had been said, meat was eaten—at least at certain times—and the inedible remainders were not carelessly thrown away, since these also had been blessed. To this day devout Jews do not throw away prayer books or ritual objects when they are old and worn out, but rather bury them or deposit them in a so-called Genizah. For a closer picture of the Qumrân community the cemetery is also of special interest. The graves in the cemetery to the east are all, with a single exception, placed in a north-south direction; here without exception the skeletons are male. There are no articles of any kind in the graves. A single definitely female grave in this plot is not placed in the same direction as the others and is of a different kind. Farther to the east was found another cemetery in which the graves were not so carefully arranged and are oriented in various directions. Here there were also graves of women and children and in two women's graves there were found one bronze ring, nineteen fossilized pearls, and two earrings. North and south of Qumrân further graves were found, here again including those of women and children. In one woman's grave there were two earrings and thirty pearls. It follows therefore that monks were apparently buried in the large cemetery to the east of the monastery building, whereas the married members of the community, including women, were buried in a separate place. The findings of these excavations fit in well with the content of the text, since the Manual of Discipline contains the statutes of a monastic community whereas the Book of Rules presents regulations for the married.

The findings of the excavations in regard to the inhabitants of the settlement and the geographical situation of Khirbet Qumrân remind us of the account of Pliny the Elder (*Naturalis Historia* 5, 17) in which he states that the Jewish group of Essenes lived a common life without women and without money beneath the palms on the west side of the Dead Sea in the neighbourhood of Engedi. When we consider that very many of the regulations of the Manual of Discipline and the Damascus Document reveal far-reaching similarities with the accounts of Philo of Alexandria and Josephus Flavius concerning the Essenes' way of life we are forced to conclude that this community, must be included in the broader complex of Essene groups (cf. Chap. VIII).

The excavations in Qumrân revealed the following levels:

Level Ia: The community building was erected, upon foundation walls that date from the eighth century, in the second part of the reign of John Hyrcanus (135-104 B.C.), at which time the community had to be satisfied with extremely modest facilities.

Level Ib: During the reign of Alexander Janneus (103–76 B.C.) the community received new impetus and may well have experienced its heyday throughout this whole period, represented by Level Ib. In the year 31 B.C. the building was destroyed by an earthquake and in consequence was abandoned.

Level II: Not until the reign of Herod Archelaus (4.B.C. to A.D. 6) was the building restored by adherents of the same community and it stood until June, A.D. 68, when Vespasian marched with the Roman Tenth Legion from Caesarea to Jericho and thus also reached the Dead Sea. On this occasion the monastery was destroyed. The texts may have been hidden in the caves immediately before this.

The Roman troops occupied the buildings, but allowed the greater part of the water system to deteriorate and filled up some of the cisterns with rubble. This indicates that the period of occupation no longer has any connection with our community, which for ritual reasons set great store upon the water system and the cisterns. After the site was abandoned by the Roman troops and had remained uninhabited for some time it was used for a brief time during the Second Jewish Revolt, A.D. 132–5, as a partisan base by the followers of Bar Kokhba.

The dating of the building and the individual levels is made possible by the ceramics found there and the various reconstructions undertaken during the several building periods as well as unusually rich finds of coins. The oldest coins discovered are from the time of John Hyrcanus and a large number come from the time of Alexander Jannaeus. The coins then extend to the first years of the reign of Herod the Great. The earthquake, which can be dated, through an account of Josephus Flavius, as occurring in the year 31 B.C., was the cause of a gap in the occupation of the site which is thus also confirmed by the evidence of the coins. Traces of this earthquake are also recognizable in the ruins of the monastery. After this gap there are no coins until the time of Herod Archelaus, which extend to the third year of the Jewish-Roman war, namely the year A.D. 68–9. A deposit of silver coins was also found which may possibly have nothing to do with the community and merely be the cache of a man who buried his treasure there during the time when the building was abandoned on account of the destruction caused by the earthquake. The place at which the silver coins were found was not entirely cleared up after the resumption of occupation in the second period and the floor of this period was laid over it. Moreover, two of the pots in which the deposit of silver coins was found are of a form which bears no relationship to the usual ceramics discovered in Qumrân.

Thus the results of the excavations also point to the time between 120 B.C. and A.D. 68 and we should date the community's main period of florescence somewhere between

100 and 50 B.C. This fits well with the most probable dating of the Teacher of Righteousness in the time of Alexander Jannaeus.

VI

THE PREDECESSORS OF THE ESSENE COMMUNITY OF KHIRBET QUMRÂN

I. IN THE POST-EXILIC PERIOD

a) *The Priestly Tradition*

THE Qumrân community had a priestly head. The priests of the community are called either "sons of Aaron" (e.g., Manual of Discipline 9, 7) or "sons of Zadok" (e.g., Book of Rules 1, 24). As with the Sadducees, it was therefore necessary for the Qumrân priests to derive their genealogy from the priest Zadok. According to II Sam. 8:17; 15:24; 20:25; I Kings 1:8, Zadok, along with Abiathar, was a priest at the time of David, and Solomon appointed him priest in place of Abiathar (I Kings 2:35). In post-exilic times membership of the house of Zadok was a prerequisite of legitimate priestly office. In Ezekiel's vision of the new temple only the sons of Zadok are to have the right to make sacrifices (Ezek. 40:46) and in 44:15 it is specifically stated that "the Levitical priests, the sons of Zadok, who kept the charge of my sanctuary when the people of Israel went astray from me, shall come near to me to minister to me; and they shall attend on me to offer me the fat and blood, says the Lord JHWH". Also in the lists of priests in I Chron. 6:1—15 and 6:49–53 the name of Zadok occurs in the same dominant position in the ancestral line which is absolutely necessary for legitimate priesthood. When, for reasons which will be considered in detail later, the Qumrân priests dissociated

28

themselves from the Jerusalem cult which was administered by priests who in their eyes were impure, they were preparing themselves, as the second column of the War Scroll and other passages show, for a cultus in the eschatological era which was to be administered by them, the sole legitimate descendants of Zadok. Professor Ethelbert Stauffer classified the Qumrân texts within the larger context of a priestly tradition which in his opinion extends from the priestly code to John the Baptist and the Johannine school in Ephesus (E. Stauffer, *Probleme der Priestertradition, ThLZ* 81, 1956, 135–50.)

b) *The Two-Messiahs Doctrine*

The heads of the post-exilic community were at first a Zadokite priest, Joshua, the son of Jehozadak (according to I Chron: 6:15 Jehozadak was sent into exile by Nebuchadnezzar) and, officiating with him, a Davidic governer, Zerubbabel, the son of Salathiel (according to I Chron. 3:17 Salathiel belongs to the house of David). Just as David, in the view of the Chronicler, was, by reason of the preparations he made for the building of the temple and the service of the temple, the real builder of the first temple, whose work was merely completed by Solomon, so the Branch of David (Zech. 3:8; 6:12), Zerubbabel, is considered to be the builder of the second temple (Zech. 4:9). It was probably not until concrete messianic hopes were associated with the person of Zerubbabel (Hag. 2: 20–23) that he was removed by the central Persian government. In any case after him no Davidic governor was installed and both the secular and the spiritual authority was combined in the hands of the high priest. Zechariah 6:9–13 then represents in the contemporary setting an attempt to meet this new situation and to regularize it. Both crowns were placed upon the head of Joshua, the son of Jehozadak, the high priest (Zech. 6:11). This situation created by the external political circumstances of the time is not, however, the final one; in the messianic period the ideal division of the office into two is to be reintroduced. Then, along with the messianic high priest, there shall arise a new Branch of David (Zech. 6:12), who, according to Jer. 23:5 and 33:15, is undoubtedly to be identified with the messianic Davidic King. "It is he who shall build the temple of JHWH, and shall bear royal honour, and shall sit and rule upon his throne. And there shall be a priest by his throne and peaceful understanding shall be between them both" (Zech. 6:13). The messianic concept may therefore have been somewhat as follows: just as the erection of the first temple can be traced back to David and Zadok so that of the second temple goes back to Zerubbabel and Joshua, the son of Jehozadak. But these themselves became, after the non-fulfilment of the messianic hopes connected with Zerubbabel, patterns for the real messianic age. Zechariah 3:8 and the prophecy concerning the two "sons of oil", i.e., anointed ones, messiahs, in Zech 4:11–14 also belong in this context. The doctrine that in the eschatological age a priestly and a Davidic Messiah would rule jointly now became a central theologumenon in the Essene Qumrân community (cf. chap X). Thus in this respect too the concepts of the Qumrân texts have concretely ascertainable antecedents in post-exilic biblical writings.

c) *Influences in the Works of the Chronicler*

The most striking characteristic of the Chronicler's historical work is that it is in unusual degree both pro-Zadokite and pro-Davidic. The story of David's youth and, above all, unfavourable episodes in his life, such, as, for example, the Bathsheba affair, are suppressed by the Chronicler. Instead, however, he expatiates upon David as the real architect of the first temple and the organizer of the cultus in a way that goes far beyond the account of II Samuel (cf. J. M. Grintz, *The Life of David in Samuel and Chronicles* [hebr.], Beth Mikra I, 1956, pp. 69–75; J. Botterweck, "Zur Eigenart der chronistischen Davidgeschichte", *Festchrift für Viktor Christian*, Vienna. 1956, pp. 12–31). The genealogies of priests with their special esteem for the priest Zadok, mentioned in section (a), are also characteristic of the Chronicler's style. Thus David is already described by him as the prototype of the Messiah and builder of the temple, along with whom the Zadokite-priestly element then plays the determining role in the real formation of the cultus. The assumption of a messianic high priest and a messianic Branch of David as the builder of the temple, which is characteristic of Zechariah's theology, may also be responsible for this characteristic feature of the Chronicler's historical writing.

2. THE MOVEMENT OF THE "PIOUS" IN THE MACCABEAN PERIOD

At the beginning of the second century before Christ there sprang up in Palestine a group of extremely religious Jews who were prompted by the sinfulness of their time to believe in an imminent end of the age. The writer of the Book of Daniel may well have been one of these. Those chapters of the Book of Daniel which contain an apocalyptic theology of history (chaps. 2 and 7–12) point in particular to this milieu. Calculations concerning the duration of the last age and the appointed day of the end were first begun in these circles which were imbued with an

eschatological, messianic expectation. The later apocalypticism is connected with them both intellectually and
historically.

These people were called Hasidim, the "godly ones",
the "Pious" by their contemporaries. Later rabbinical
writings call them *Hasidim rishonim*, the "earlier Pious". In
both of the Books of Maccabees the Hebrew term *"Hasidim"* is rendered by the Greek form *asidaioi*. Because of
their piety they are also referred to in the rabbinical
sources as *'anshe ma'ase*, "men of Deeds". These *Hasidim*
set themselves apart from the sinful world around them
and lived in the caves of the desert of Judah (I Macc.
2:29, 31, 41). The somewhat later Qumrân texts show that
they fled into the desert not only to be safe from the Syrian
intervention troops but also because they regarded the
desert as the place of salvation where the divine redemption would first reveal itself. Isaiah 40:3 may well have
brought about such an attitude. In any case the Manual of
Discipline of Qumrân 8:12–14 says, "when they join themselves together into a community in Israel in conformity
with these regulations they must separate themselves from
the dwelling place of sinners and go to the wilderness to
prepare there the way of the LORD, as it is written, 'In
the wilderness prepare the way of the LORD, make
straight in the desert a highway for our God' ". Also in the
War Scroll 1:2 the community itself is called a "desert
emigration". Even the choice of the site northwest of the
Dead Sea in the desert of Judah for the monastery of
Qumrân and also the sojourn of John the Baptist in the
desert may have been partly determined by such con-
siderations.

We have only very scanty sources for the history of these
Hasidim and their actual way of life and yet the Qumrân

texts permit a good many, albeit cautious, conclusions. Originally, as I Macc. 2:29–42 indicates, they probably had no connection with the revolt of Mattathias, but they were very closely in sympathy with the rebels because both groups were concerned with the restoration of the religious order. Under Judas Maccabaeus, with whose appearance the *Hasidim* associated their apocalyptical, eschatological ideals, at any rate some of them may have been counted among his loyal followers (II Macc. 14:6). This may also be the sense in which the apocalypse of the sheep in chapter 90 of the Book of Enoch is to be understood: "9. And I saw till horns grew upon the lambs, and the ravens cast down their horns; and I saw till there sprouted a great horn (i.e. Judas) of one of those sheep (i.e., Mattathias), and their eyes were opened. . . . 12. And those ravens fought and battled with it and sought to lay low its horn, but they had no power over it". Also the statement of Alcimus to Demetrius I that the Asidaioi were great wagers of war (II Macc. 14:6) may not, according to Enoch 90:19, be incorrect: "And I saw till a great sword was given to the sheep, and the sheep proceeded against all the beasts of the field to slay them, and all the beasts and the birds of heaven fled before their face". The concept of an eschatological war of revenge waged by the righteous elect against their enemies and the enemies of God is evidenced in other passages in the Book of Enoch as well as in the Qumrân texts. The motives however, which prompted the *Hasidim* and the Maccabees to take up arms were different. Whereas the *Hasidim* hoped for the eschatological establishment of the kingdom of God the Maccabees were satisfied with securing religious freedom and achieving it politically and militarily and in time even came to engage in wholly profane power politics.

The *Hasidim*, however, were not interested in this on account of their generally eschatological point of view. For this reason they also made peace with the high priest Alcimus, who was of Aaronic priestly descent, and his protector, the Syrian general Bacchides (I Macc. 7:12–15). Nevertheless their hopes were not fulfilled and Bacchides executed sixty of them (7:16). This actually exhausts our information about the *Hasidim* and yet we know from the Qumrân texts, from the early rabbinical literature, and from Josephus Flavius that during the subsequent period both of the "parties" which arose from the *Hasidim* movement, the Essene group as well as the Pharisees, increasingly dissociated themselves from the Maccabean-Hasmonean dynasty for one reason or another.

The Old Testament law was observed by the *Hasidim* with extraordinary strictness. According to I Macc. 2:32, 36, 38, they even refused to defend themselves against their enemies and take up arms on the sabbath. An interesting parallel from the realm of the Qumrân Essenes is provided by the War Scroll 2:8 f., in which it is said, with reference to the war in its last period of forty years: "In the sabbath years, however, there is to be no mustering for warfare, for that is a sabbath of rest for Israel". The Damascus Document also records a very rigorous observance of the sabbath in these circles, even to the disregard for saving life. "If any person falls into a cistern or into a pool on the sabbath, one must not bring him up by means of a ladder, or rope, or other instrument" (11:16 f.). In Niddah 38a a Baraita (i.e. a Tannaitic teaching, before A.D. 200) says of the *Hasidim Rišhonim* that even in the begetting of children they were careful not to choose a date which would result in a probable birth on the sabbath, since they consider even birth a desecration of the sabbath. According to Shabbat 121b, they would not even kill snakes and scorpions on the sabbath. A very strict observance of the sabbath in the circles of the *Hasidim* is therefore relatively well attested. In any case it is apparent that in this matter they were much stricter than were the later Pharisees, for whom "any danger to life superseded the sabbath" (Yoma 8:6, and who therefore also made it permissible to help a woman in childbirth and allowed a midwife to travel from one place to another for this purpose (Shabbat 18:3).

Berakot 5:1 states that they devoted an hour to getting into the right attitude for prayer. After praying for an hour they remained in the same attitude for another hour (Berakot 32b). According to a Baraita transmitted in Baba Kamma 30a, they usually buried thorns and pieces of broken glass in such a way that they would no longer be obstacles to a plough. In Sukkah 5:4 some special hymns are mentioned which are said to be familiar in the circles of the *Hasidim rišhonim*. Perhaps the hymns in the Hymn Scroll of Qumrân are similar liturgical poems from the circle of the Qumrân Essenes.

VII

THE ORIGIN OF THE ESSENE COMMUNITY OF KHIRBET QUMRÂN AND ITS RELATIONSHIP TO THE PHARISEES AND SADDUCEES

THE driving force which led to the formation of the *Hasidim* movement was the eschatological expectation and the knowledge that the temple services in Jerusalem were being administered by impure and sinful priests. Therefore both priests and laymen found themselves together in the movement for somewhat different reasons. They were at one in rejecting the assimilation policy of the Syrian kings and their interference in the internal affairs of the Jews, which provided influential positions for the apostate Jews. The priests within the *Hasidim* movement also considered the sacrifices which were offered by the impure priests in Jerusalem as an abomination to God and besides this they may also have stood for a different calendar and order of holy days (cf. chap. VIII, 3 d).

We have already mentioned an initial estrangement between the *Hasidim* and Judas and his brothers occasioned by the installation of Alcimus into office (I Macc. 7:10–14). Later, when the Maccabean-Hasmonean kings continued to pursue exclusively profane and political aims, they were definitely rejected by the followers of the *Hasidim* who continued to think in eschatological, apocalyptic terms. *But these followers are the people about whom the Qumrân texts bear witness* and from whose milieu they come. At the latest the opposition to the Hasmoneans probably occurred on the basis of the plebiscite of the year 141 B.C., when Simon and his descendants were accorded the highest spiritual and secular rank by the people (I Macc. 14:41). At the time of Alexander Janneus (103–76 B.C.), when the Qumrân community was also in its first fine flowering (cf. end of chap. V), the contest with the Hasmoneans reached its peak.

The Qumrân community itself was at its core a priestly community. Dissident priests of the house of Zadok (cf. chap. VI, 1, a) constituted its centre. In addition, laymen too belonged essentially to the community which considered itself "a holy house for Israel, a foundation of the holy of holies for Aaron" (Manual of Discipline 8:5f.).

However, not only the Qumrân Essenes but also the Pharisees had their origin in the movement of the *Hasidim.* Among them, though, the priests did not occupy such a dominant position as in the Qumrân community. In any case they were not so highly organized. One might rather class the Pharisees as democratic, since different interpretations of the law were possible among them and were held in great respect even when they were contradictory. Such an attitude would have been impossible among the Qumrân Essenes since the individual member was compelled to render absolute obedience to the government and also since the prophecies of the Teacher of Righteousness were regarded as binding for the faith (Hab. Com. 8:1–3). The most important mark of distinction between the two groups, however, may well have been their differing attitude towards the near apocalyptic expectation. The Qumrân Essenes clung to the messianic hopes of the *Hasidim* despite the fact that the first expectations were not fulfilled. The Qumrân texts themselves give evidence not only of the non-fulfilment of these expectations but also of the fact that these hopes were cherished in spite of all disappointments. The Pharisees, however, had through experience become sceptical in these matters. Indicative of this is the fact that not a single messianic pronouncement can be documented from Tannaitic-Pharisaic circles in the period preceding the destruction of Jerusalem in the year A.D. 70, whereas the pseudepigrapha of this period are full of such utterances. In the New Testament too the Pharisees appear to be sceptical rather than receptive to the message of the imminent kingdom of God. Particularly paradigmatic of the Pharisaic attitude too is the speech of Gamaliel I in the Sanhedrin, Acts 5:34–9.

Thus the Pharisees separated themselves from the priestly fanatics of the law in Qumrân and their acute messianic expectation, and it may well have been for this reason that they were called *pherushim*, separated ones, dissidents. The Habakkuk Commentary accordingly also calls them *bogdim*, "apostates". Since the Pharisees are documented as a group as early as the reign of John Hyrcanus (135–104 B.C.), with whom they fell out (Josephus, *Ant.* 13, 10, 5, 6; Kiddushim 66a), they must have made their appearance at this time at the latest as a more or less clearly defined group, consisting essentially of scholars of the law.

The Sadducees owe their name to the priestly family of Zadok (cf. chap. VI, 1, a). Thus from the point of view of descent their priests belonged to the same family as the priests of the Qumrân Essenes, but in attitude and thought there was a deep cleavage between them. The Sadducaic priests belonged to the liberal aristocracy and they not only rejected the apocalyptic speculations, the angelology, and the doctrine of resurrection of their revisionist priestly colleagues but they did not recognize the so-called "oral Torah" of the Pharisees either, i.e., the Pharisaic accommodation of the law to the new circumstances of the time. In this sense one may in some ways describe the Sadducees as the descendants of the Hellenists, though they had given up the most radical of the demands.

We arrive therefore at the following general picture of the Jewish groups in the period from 200 B.C. to A.D. 70. After Antiochus III took Palestine from the Ptolemies in 198 B.C. and added it to his great Syrian empire it was not long before Syrian interference in the internal Jewish self-government in Jerusalem took place. This action on the part of the Syrians was approved by those Jewish groups which were interested in an external accommodation of Judaism to the Hellenistic, syncretistic spirit of the times. To Jews who were loyal to the tradition, no matter of what kind, this attitude must of necessity have appeared to be apostasy from the religion of the fathers. Some extremists, whose core—at least at a later date when the Qumrân community was already in existence—probably consisted of dissident priests of the house of Zadok, felt that this evil state of affairs was a sure sign that it could not go on for long and that God himself would soon intervene to put an end to such goings-on. This may probably have been the origin of the apocalpytic, eschatological expectations of an imminent end. Because these people lived in expectation of the coming kingdom of God, they observed the law with special strictness and, as the Qumrân people did later, considered themselves to be an elect community of penitents, those who had repented of sinfulness (e.g., Hymn Scroll, Plate 2, 9). These "pious ones", who originally had nothing to do with the Maccabean

movement, attached themselves to it at first and during
the time of religious persecution (168–164 B.C.) apparently
expected that, with the re-establishment of the cultus, the
eschatological event would also occur (cf. the figures given
in Daniel 7:25; 8:14; 9:27; 12:7, 11–13, all of which
envisage a period of about three and a half years). When
this failed to occur they may have continued to expect it
to happen in the very near future (cf. chap. VI, 2).

When these hopes too were disappointed many gave up
their expectation of an imminent messianic age and sought
to reconcile a life of faithfulness to the law with a continuing existence in the world. These became known in the
sources as Pharisees. Others, however, believed that, despite all the delays, the last age was near at hand, "for the
ultimate end is protracted . . . and all the end periods of
God will come in their order, as he has [pre-]determined
for them in the mysteries of his wisdom" (Hab. Com.
7:7–14). Those, then, who had come to terms with the
continuance of the present aeon appeared to them to be
the "apostates of the end of days . . . who do not believe
when they hear all the things that are to come upon the
last generation" (Hab. Com. 2:5–7). Thus there arose the
Essenic groups and the Pharisees, between whom, according to the Qumrân texts, there was a complete lack of
understanding, although both were in opposition to the
Hasmonean dynasty which had allied itself with the
Sadducees.

Though the apocalyptic mentality had its origin in the
Hasidim of the Maccabean period and then in the Qumrân
community, all of the apocalpytic groups cannot simply
be classed with the Qumrân Essenes. In this connection it
is significant that in all ten of the Enoch manuscripts from
Cave IV, the section of Similitudes, which is rich in

apocalyptic visions, is missing (cf. chap. I, 3, b). Thus it is highly probable that there were apocalpytic, ecshatological expectations outside the Qumrân group. The mass of Jewry, which was neither Pharisaic nor Sadducaic in the intertestamental period, was not a solid unity. Those groups which certainly differed among themselves are best described in the New Testament expression as those who were waiting for "the kingdom of God". Despite the new finds, the source material is still much too scanty for more detailed definitions. In the wider scope of these messianic, eschatological movements we must also include the circle of John the Baptist (cf. chap. XI, 1) and the Zealots. It is impossible, however, to make any precise statements particularly with regard to relationships with the latter.

VIII

THE ESSENE COMMUNITY OF
KHIRBET QUMRÂN

ONE of the most important sources for the Essenes' way of life is the historian Josephus Flavius, who says in the second chapter of his autobiography that he himself spent some time among the Essenes. Besides these, there are also valuable accounts in Philo of Alexandria and a brief reference in Pliny, *Naturalis Historia* 5, 17. In addition there are a few references by church writers. These sources, the reliability of which has sometimes been seriously doubted, have been largely confirmed by the Qumrân texts. And yet not only agreements but also discrepancies can be detected. Thus the Qumrân texts contain many conceptions (e.g., covenant, eschatological expectation, Teacher of Righteousness) which are missing in the accounts of Philo and Josephus concerning the Essenes. On the other hand, these authors also record a number of details concerning the living habits of the Essenes for which no documentation can be found in the Qumrân texts. The discrepancies are partly explained by the fact that the ancient authors were writing for a Gentile or an assimilated, Hellenized Jewish public, which did not understand many of the Jewish ideas of the Essenes or was offended by them. Thus, for example, in Josephus the Essene hope in resurrection became belief in the immortality of the soul (*Bellum* 2, 8, 11; *Ant.* 18, 1, 5) of which even the ancient heathen could have some understanding. For the sake of these conceptions, Philo and Josephus, too, may have passed over in silence the apocalyptic, eschatological ideals. On the other hand, the differences between the teachings of the Qumrân texts and the ancient accounts concerning the Essenes may be attributable to the difference in time between most of the Qumrân texts and Philo and Josephus as well as to the fact that Essenism consisted of a number of groups, some of which were not uniformly organized.

I. THE NON-MONASTIC GROUP

After giving a detailed account of the monastic Essenes, Josephus also mentions another branch of this community, "who agree with the rest as to their way of living, and customs, and laws, but differ from them in the point of marriage". This group did not reject procreation on principle, but it too lived in conformity with the general Essenic ideal of continence and condemned all sexual lust. We may cite first as evidence of this in the sphere of the Qumrân community the fact that, as well as the great main cemetery, the graves of women and children were found (cf. chap. V). The Book of Rules also mentions women and children, contains regulations regarding the age of majority, and states very definitely that no male member of the community may marry until he has reached the age of twenty (1:10). The Damascus Document, too, at any rate partially assumes the practice of marriage (7:6a–9). Those passages in the Damascus Document which recognize private property may also have applied to the non-monastic adherents of the community (9:10–16; 11:12; cf. chap. VIII., 2, a).

43

2. THE MONASTIC GROUP

a) Requirements for Admission to the Community

The Essene monastic community recognized postulant-ship, novitiate, and full membership. According to Josephus (*Bellum* 2, 8, 7), the postulant had to "undergo for one year outside the order the same way of life as that of the members". The Manual of Discipline also recognizes this precept, but it does not indicate how long the postulancy should last. In 6:13–15 we read; "Everyone from Israel who desires voluntarily to join the 'council of the community' is to be examined by the superintendent, who is at the head of the full members, with respect to his understanding and his works and, if he is capable of discipline, he shall permit him to enter the covenant to turn back to the truth and to turn away from all error. Then he shall instruct him in all the ordinances of the community".

Concerning the two-year novitiate which follows this, Josephus says, "When he has passed the test of continence during this period of time he approaches one step nearer to the fellowship. He participates in the purifying consecration with water, but he is still not admitted to the common meals; for after he has demonstrated his constancy his character is tested for two more years and only if he appears worthy in this respect also is he formally admitted to the order" (*Bellum* 2, 8, 7). The Manual of Discipline gives more precise particulars regarding the two novitiate years: "Then, when he comes in to stand before the full members [after the postulantship], they shall all be questioned concerning him, and according

44

as to the full members decide concerning him he is admitted or rejected. If he is admitted to the 'council of the community', he still may not touch the purity of the full members until they have tested his understanding and his works for a full year. Moreover, he may still not have any part in the wealth of the full members. And, when he has thus completed a year within the community, the full members shall take counsel concerning him with respect to his understanding and his deeds in the Torah. And if it is decided concerning him to admit him to the community according to the word of the priests and the majority of the men of their covenant, his wealth and his working capacity shall be delivered to the man who is the overseer of the work of the full members. He shall enter it into a special account and shall not yet disburse it for the full members. He himself dare not touch the drink of the full members until he has completed a second full year among the men of the community. And when he has completed this second year he shall be examined according to the word of the full members, and if it is decided concerning him to admit him to the community, he shall be registered in the order of his rank among the brethren, for the Torah and the Law as well as for purity and the sharing of goods. Thus his counsel and his judgment now belong to the community" (6:15–23).

It is noteworthy that there is nothing in these provisions for admittance concerning the "purifying consecration with water" mentioned by Josephus, but that otherwise there is broad agreement. On the other hand, however, it is known from the findings of the excavations at Khirbet Qumrân (cf. chap. V) that the community placed high value upon purification by water and manifestly was also familiar with ritual baths (cf. chap. VIII, 3, b).

Josephus says further in the same account: "Meanwhile, however, before he is allowed to appear at the common meal, he must take a tremendous oath before the members of the order that he will honour God, fulfil his obligations to men . . . , always hate the unrighteous and help the righteous, and that he will show fidelity to all men and especially to those in authority . . . . Furthermore he must swear, in case he himself should ever be in authority, never to vaunt his power, nor endeavour to outshine his subjects either in his garments or any other finery. He further binds himself always to love the truth and destroy falsehood, to keep his hands clean from theft and his soul from the stain of unlawful gains, to conceal nothing from the brethren of the order, to reveal none of their secrets to others even though he were to be tortured to death; and finally, never to communicate the doctrines of the order to anybody except in the way in which he himself learned to know them, to abhor highway robbery, and to keep secret the books of the sect and the names of the angels".

Admittedly the Manual of Discipline 6:20 does not speak in express terms of a "common meal", but it does speak of the "drink of the full members" which the novice dare not touch even in the last year of his novotiate. Nevertheless, common meals, which apparently had a ritual character, are also mentioned in the Qumrân texts (cf. chap. VIII, 3, a), and the excavation findings show too that the Qumrân community had a large community refectory (cf. chap. V). The provisions of the vow of the order—reverence to God, hatred of sinners, and aid to the righteous—are formulated very similarly in the Manual of Discipline 1:2–4: ". . . to do what is good and upright before him as he commanded through Moses and all his servants the prophets; to love all whom he has chosen and to hate all whom he has rejected." The strict hierarchical organization of the community, which is confirmed especially in the Manual of Discipline (e.g., 5:23), can be viewed as parallel to Josephus' statement that the Essenes were obliged to render obedience to the superiors of the order. In this connection reference may be made to the committee of twelve laymen and three priests mentioned in the Manual of Discipline 8:1, which performed a very important function in the community. Moreover, the community also recognized the office of a superintendent (e.g. Manual of Discipline 6:12, 20), an overseer (e.g., Manual of Discipline 6:14), and an instructor (e.g., Manual of Discipline 3:13; 9:12). The Book of Rules (1:24 f.; 2:16) and the War Scroll (2:1, 7) also refer to the so-called "chiefs of the fathers of the congregation". Certain administrative posts were reserved to priests, and priests and Levites had their clearly-defined functions. Thus the Manual of Discipline 9:7, for example, states that "only the sons of Aaron bear rule over judgment and wealth". The Book of Rules (2:14 f.) also refers to commanders of thousands, hundreds, fifties, tens, judges, and watchers. According to War Scroll 4:1–5, these may have had at least partially military functions.

The Qumrân texts have as yet made no reference to the equality which prevailed among the members of the sect despite the hierarchical rule of the order, an equality in which the superiors were not distinguished from the others by any sort of clothing or ornaments, though possibly we may cite for comparison the fact that in the large cemetery to the east of Qumrân only male skeletons without any ornaments whatsoever were found (cf. chap. V).

According to Josephus, the Essene novice had to vow

"to keep his soul clear from the stain of unlawful gain". The Manual of Discipline (1:11 f.,) likewise states that "all who voluntarily confess his truth must bring all their knowledge, their strength, and their wealth into the community of God". The Manual of Discipline 6:19 also speaks of the surrender of property in connection with the regulations concerning the reception of novices and the prayer in 10:19 reads, "I have no desire for sinful wealth". In this connection also belongs the statement that community of goods was generally practiced at least in the monastic part of the community. Josephus says in this connection in *Bellum* 2, 8, 3, "There is a law among them that everyone who desires to join the sect must assign his wealth to the whole"; and in *Ant.* 18, 1, 5 he reports that they practiced "complete community of goods". This is a clear parallel to the passage in the Manual of Discipline 1:11 f., quoted above. Philo too gives an account of the Essenes' practice of community of goods in his treatise *"Quod omnis probus liber sit"*, chap. 12, and also in his "Apology for the Jews" (Eusebius, *Praeparatio Evangelica*, 8, 11). How far complete community of goods was practiced by the married (and perhaps also many unmarried) members of the community we do not know, since the Damascus Document takes private property for granted (e.g., 9:10–16). Indeed, Dam. Doc. 14: 12–14 requires of the full members only the payment of at least two day's wages per month for communal purposes. This difficulty cannot be overcome by assuming that there was a development in the history of the community from private ownership to community ownership. It is certain, however, that voluntarily assumed poverty was regarded as a prerequisite of a God-pleasing life, indeed, even as a state of grace (cf. chap. IX, 1, b).

According to Josephus' account, the Essenes were required never to conceal anything from the members of the order, but to observe strict secrecy with everyone else. Similarly, concerning the conduct of the righteous man, the Manual of Discipline 4:5 f. states, that he is "to constrain himself to walking in prudence in all things and to concealing for truth the secrets of wisdom". Even more clearly, it is stated in 9:17 that "the counsel of the Torah must be concealed from sinners, but knowledge of the truth and righteous judgment must be taught to those who choose the right way". The Essene's duty to be steadfast "even though he were to be tortured to death" had a parallel in the Manual of Discipline 1:16–18, "All who come into the order of the community shall enter into the covenant before God, to do all that he has commanded, and not to turn away from him because of fear, dread, terror, or threat in the time of the dominion of Belial". The books of the sect which Josephus mentions were probably the pseudepigrapha which were disseminated in the community and which also contain many angelological sections.

This detailed comparison of the requirements for admission to the Qumrân community with the corresponding account of Josephus concerning admission to Essenism may well lead the reader to the conclusion that the Qumrân fellowship should be included within the broader circle of Essene groups.

b) The Discipline of the Community

According to the Manual of Discipline 2:9 the covenant obligations were apparently reviewed each year and recalled to the remembrance of the members in the course of a solemn ceremony. Anyone who violated them was faced with various degrees of punishment which stipulated penitential periods ranging from ten days, thirty days, three months, six months, one and two years, to complete exclusion (Manual of Discipline 6:24–9:2). Josephus also reports in *Bellum* 2, 8, 8, that grievous sinners were cast out, but sometimes readmitted out of compassion.

c) *The Rules of the Order*

In his early treatise *"Quod omnis probus liber sit"*, chap. 12, Philo reports that the Essenes cultivated philosophy, not as logic and physics, but rather as ethics, and this in dependence upon the laws of the fathers revealed by God. "These they study at all times, but particularly on the Sabbath, which they keep holy by abstaining from work and gathering in hallowed places. There they sit in order of age and listen as one of them reads from the books and another, more learned, expounds whatever is not understood by teaching them to comprehend it as a symbol and bringing out its deeper meaning. Similarly, the Manual of Discipline 6:8 f. says, "This is the seating order for the full members, each in his order. First the priests are seated, the elders in second place, and the rest of the people shall be seated, each in his order". Manual of Discipline 6:6 f. appears to point to the office of a scribe in a passage which prescribes that in a community of at least ten members there must be one man who is constantly studying the Torah. The Habbakuk Commentary and similar writings make it abundantly clear that the believers of Qumrân interpreted the Bible symbolically.

Concerning the meetings of the Essenes we read in Josephus, *Bellum* 2,8,5, "that neither clamour nor other disturbance desecrates their house, but each allows the other to speak in his turn", and in *Bellum* 2,8,9, "that they consider it honourable to render obedience to age and to the majority "and "that if ten of them are sitting together, no one of them will speak against the opinion of the other nine". This may be compared with Manual of Discipline 6:10 f.: "A man dare not speak in the midst of his brother's words, before his brother has finished speaking. And further he shall not speak before his turn comes as it is written before him".

From the passages cited, Manual of Discipline 6:6 and *Bellum* 2,8,9, as well as Manual of Discipline 6:3, and the Book of Rules 2:22, where it is prescribed that the rule applies to common meals (cf. chap. VIII, 3, a) when ten members are together, it may follow that at least ten members were necessary for common religious exercises. Modern orthodox Judaism also recognizes the precept that no congregational prayer can be spoken without *minjan*, i.e., ten men. Manual of Discipline 10:1–8 also contains a fixed order of prayer. Each day prayers are spoken "at the beginning of the dominion of light [i.e., at terce], at the high point of its circuit [i.e., at sext], and when it returns to its fixed place [i.e., at nones], at the beginning of the night watches when he opens his treasury [i.e., at evening] . . . at the high point of the circuit of the night [i.e., at midnight] and when it [night] withdraw before the rising light [i.e., at dawn]." Corresponding to the course of the day, the monthly prayers were also regulated according to the pattern of beginning, middle, and end: "at the beginning of the festival seasons for the days of the month, also when they have reached their high point and when they pass one over into the other". Special prayers were said on holy days and special regulations for prayer applied to the various seasons of the year.

The statutes of the fellowship also contain the following

main points: No one dare bring any complaint against his neighbour to the plenary meeting if he has not previously reproved him in the presence of witnesses. The members eat, pray, and take council together. They must watch, pray, and study the Scriptures for one-third of the night. There are a number of specific, individual precepts, but space does not permit us to cite them here.

3. THE TEACHINGS OF THE QUMRÂN ESSENES

a) The Communal Meal

Special difficulties are created by the interpretation of the Essene communal meal which many scholars have connected with the Christian Lord's Supper. Josephus reports in *Bellum* 2,8,5: "After the purification, they repair to a special building . . . and now purified they assemble . . . in the refectory. . . . Before the meal begins, the priest says a prayer and no one is allowed to eat anything before the prayer. After the meal he prays again". Such a refectory with an adjoining room for dishes has been excavated in the ruins of Qumrân and it is very probable that the tile-paved circle which is discernible there indicates the place of the presiding priest (cf. chap. V). The Manual of Discipline 6:4–6 also speaks of such a meal: "When they seat themselves at table to eat or to drink wine, the priest shall first stretch forth his hand in order first to bless bread and wine and to eat". In the Book of Rules 2:11–21 the same meal is described, but in this case as it will take place in the messianic age under the presidency of the Priest-Messiah. According to Josephus (*Bellum* 2,8,7), only the full member is allowed to participate in the common meals and according to the Manual of Discipline 6:20, the novice is still not to touch the drink of the full members.

During the excavations in Qumrân, ossuaries containing the bones of animals which had been cooked or roasted were discovered in places which had not been roofed over. The theory that these are the bones of animals over which a blessing had been said before their flesh was eaten, the remains of which would also be subject to the sacred effects of this blessing, seems very natural. So they were buried in ossuaries, since consecrated bones could not be carelessly thrown away.

This fact has led many to the premature inference of seeing in the "Essene meal" a prototype of the Christian Eucharist. According to all that can be found in the texts, however, such a theory cannot be justified. It is true here that the food and drink appear to be blessed, in a certain sense even consecrated, but they were not treated as signs of the establishment of the new covenant. Nor can this blessing have been connected with the person of the Messiah or with the remembrance of the Messiah, since the messianic event was still something which was expected in the future. Nevertheless, one must not disregard the fact that this meal had an arcane character, since not even the novices were permitted to participate in it, and that it was partaken of according to a strictly regulated ceremonial. It therefore cannot be characterized merely as an ordinary meal partaken of in common with table prayers. Consequently, it is true that the communal meals in the Essenic communities had a ritual character, but no sacred meaning comparable with the Christian eucharist. Yet it is undoubtedly possible that the early Christian Agape had a religious-historical connection with these meals. (Cf. K. G. Kuhn, "The Lord's Supper and the Communal Meal at Qumrân", in *The Scrolls and the New Testament*, ed., Krister Stendahl, Harper & Brothers, New York; SCM

Press, London, 1957, pp. 65–93; J. van der Ploeg, "The Meals of the Essenes", *Journal of Semitic Studies* 2[1957], pp. 163–5.)

Perhaps still another precept, contained in the Manual of Discipline 5:16 f., belongs in this context; this forbids the members of the community to accept hospitality from outsiders: "He shall not eat or drink anything that belongs to them and shall not take anything whatsoever from their hand for which he has not paid". The thought behind this precept may well have been that every possession which is not consciously placed in the service of the community is impure and therefore also makes impure anyone who accepts any of it.

b) Baths and Lustrations

Josephus states repeatedly that ritual washings were customary in Essene circles. In *Bellum* 2,8,5 we read that the Essenes washed themselves in cold water before the common meals, according to 2,8,9 they also washed themselves after relieving nature, "as if it were a defilement to them"; and also the older members are said to have washed themselves when they were touched by the younger members, "as if a foreigner had defiled them" (*Bellum* 2,8,10). The findings of the excavations in Khirbet Qumrân likewise indicate that this community attributed special value to lustrations (cf. chap. V). In the Damascus Document 10:11 it is prescribed that the water of the purification must not be dirty and must not be less than the amount which will completely cover a man. The Manual of Discipline, however, indicates that these washings were not an end in themselves, but were regarded as meaningless if they were not accompanied by a genuine turning to God. Manual of Discipline 3:4–6: "[The sinner] cannot become clean in the water of atonement and cannot sanctify himself in seas and rivers nor become clean in any kind of water for washing. Unclean, unclean shall he be so long as he rejects the ordinances of God and yields not himself to the discipline of the community of His counsel." 5:13: "[The sinner] is not allowed to enter into the water to touch the purity of the men of holiness, for one does not become pure unless one has turned from his evil".

c) Relation to the Sacrificial Cult

For a long time the relation of the Essenic groups to the sacrificial cult was very obscure. In Philo's "*Quod omnis probus liber sit*", chap. 12, we read that the piety of the Essenes was expressed, not in the sacrifice of animals, but rather in purity of mind, and Josephus (*Ant.* 18,1,5) says of the Essenes that "when they send dedicated gifts to the temple they do not offer sacrifices, because they claim to possess holier means of purification. For this reason they are not allowed entrance to the common sanctuary and accordingly they engage in their worship separately". What this account says, literally, is that the Essenes continued to recognize the Jerusalem cultus to the extent of sending dedicated gifts to the temple, but that on the other hand they had their own service of worship. As the Qumrân texts clearly indicate, the latter statement is definitely not to be understood as meaning that they practised their own sacrificial cultus.

Dissident priests of the house of Zadok may have founded the community; in any case they were certainly its hierarchical centre (cf. chap. VII). Thus from the outset it appears clear that the community must have had a clearly-defined relationship to the Jerusalem cultus. The Qumrân texts indicate that the Qumrân priests dissociated themselves completely from the Jerusalem sanctuary, because in their eyes it was served by impure priests who observed the feasts on the wrong days (cf. chap. VIII, 3, d) and without holiness of mind; but that they were waiting for the time when they themselves might again make the sacrifices in the real last days.

A clear renunciation of the Jerusalem sacrificial cultus is found in the Damascus Document 6:12: "All who enter the covenant dare not enter the sanctuary there to kindle his altar in vain". Similarly we read in the Manual of Discipline 9:3–5: "When this happens in Israel, according to all these regulations for the foundation of the spirit of holiness, for the eternal truth, [it happens] in order to atone for the sinful wickedness and the sinful apostasy and to the good pleasure [of God] for the land, more than by offerings of flesh and offerings of fat. But the offering of the lips [i.e., prayer] for justice is like delight in righteousness, and the perfect way is like a pleasing gift of sacrifice". The War Scroll 2:5 states concerning the cultus of the last age in the purified Jerusalem: "These shall preside over burnt offerings and sacrifices to prepare a pleasing odour for God's acceptance, to make atonement for all his congregation and to bring the daily sacrifice to him upon the altar of glory". This cultus in the last age may also be referred to in the Damascus Document 11:18–20: "One must not send burnt offering, meal offering, incense, and wood by the hand of a man who is unclean even in only one respect, thus permitting him to defile the altar".

Thus we have a total picture in which the community does not reject sacrifice in principle, but nevertheless for the time being dissociates itself from the Jerusalem sacrifice for the duration of the age of Belial. But when that age has passed it will itself be the priestly community of the last age. (Cf. Jean Carmignac, "L'utilité ou inutilité des sacrifices sanglants dans la Règle de la Communauté, *Revue Biblique* 63 [1956], pp. 524–32.)

d) The Calendar Problem

One of the most important reasons why the Qumrân priests rejected the sacrifice of their Jerusalem colleagues was the difference in calendrical computation. At the Jerusalem temple a lunar calendar was in force and the Qumrân Essenes used a solar calendar. Thus one would be having a Sabbath while the others would be having a weekday. According to Jubilees 6:22–38, a year of three hundred and sixty-four days, i.e., fifty-two weeks, is inscribed upon the heavenly tablets as the will of God; but 6:36–8 states that there are transgressions against this God-given order: "For there are those who will assuredly make observations of the moon—how (it) disturbs the seasons and comes in from year to year ten days too soon. For this reason the years will come upon them when they will disturb (the order), and make an abominable (day) the day of testimony, and an unclean day a feast day. . . . For this reason I command thee and testify to thee that thou mayest testify to them; for after thy death thy children will disturb (them), so that they will not make the year three hundred and sixty-four days only, and for this reason they will go wrong as to the new moons and seasons and sabbaths and festivals, and they will eat all kinds of blood with all kinds of flesh". This calendrical computation is also found in Enoch 74:10; 82:6. Both Jubilees and Enoch texts were found in the caves of Qumrân (cf. chap. II, 3, b); and the Book of Jubilees is also cited as a source in the Damascus Document 16:3 f. Thus there can be no doubt that this solar calendar was the calendar of the

57

Qumrân Essenes, who laid great stress upon "not advancing the times and not postponing any of the festival seasons" (Manual of Discipline 1:14 f.) This is also indicated by the War Scroll 2:1 f., where the number of the fathers of the community is given as fifty-two, corresponding to the number of weeks in the solar year, and the number of chiefs of the priest-guards is given as twenty-six. Twenty-six is half of fifty-two; thus each priest-guard would serve a turn for one week twice a year. The Qumrân Essenes therefore adjusted the number of priest-guards to their calendar, whereas I Chron. 24:1–18; 25:9–31, as well as the later usage (*Ant.* 7,14,7; Taanit 4:2; Taanit 27a, b), are familiar with only twenty-four priest-guards.

Considering that elsewhere in Judaism, a lunar calendar was used, the question arises as to how the Qumrân Essenes came to use a solar calendar and, what is more, to insist that this calendar was the original one. Some scholars relate the reference in Daniel 7:25, "to change the times and customs", to the fact that under Antiochus IV the lunar calendar was introduced, whereas the solar calendar is supposed to have been in use previously in the post-exilic cult-community. A clear weakness in this assumption, however, lies in the fact that it cannot explain how the Hellenists still possessed enough influence and power even after the Maccabean victories and the reconsecration of the temple in 164 B.C. to be able to enforce the retention of a foreign calendar. If the solar calendar had really been standard for the post-exilic congregation, one would hardly expect that twenty-six instead of twenty-four priest-guards would have been mentioned in Chronicles, the same as it is in the War Scroll. It is therefore at least questionable whether the solar calendar was actually in common use before the intervention of Antiochus IV.

e) *Providence and Predestination*

Not only is the solar calendar inscribed upon the heavenly tablets, but also the whole course of world history to the last judgment is recorded upon them (e.g., Jubilees 5:13). This is clearly stated in Enoch 81:1, 2: "And he said unto me: 'Observe, Enoch, these heavenly tablets and read what is written thereon and mark every individual fact. And I observed the heavenly tablets . . . of all the deeds of mankind, and of all the children of the flesh that shall be upon the earth to the remotest generations". Manual of Discipline 3:15 f. can also be understood in this sense: "From the God of knowledge is all that is and ever was and before the created things came into being he determined the order of them, and when they have come into being they fulfil their work for their testimonies according to the plan of his majesty, of which nothing is to be changed". This predestination extends to the end of the world. According to the Habakkuk Commentary 7:13 f., "the last times of God will come according to their order, even as he has [pre-]determined for them in the mysteries of his wisdom". The War Scroll 1:10 also speaks of the "day which he appointed of old for the war of destruction against the sons of darkness". It admits of no doubt that, according to the theology of the Qumrân Essenes, God's providence encompassed everything that happens in the world down to the last detail. Thus the prayer in the Hymn Scroll 1:24 reads: "Everything is engraved before thee in a tablet of remembrance for all everlasting times and the periods of the number of the years of the world in all the times appointed for them".

Human destiny, too, is largely determined by divine

providence. According to Josephus, *Ant.* 13,5,9, the Essenes taught "that everything is subject to the power of fate and nothing happens to man which is not determined by destiny". In the Hymn Scroll 4:29 f. we read that "man lives in iniquity from the womb" and he who is able to go the right way is illuminated by God for his covenant (4:5). Hence the members of the sect called themselves *bene rashon*, "sons of [divine] good pleasure" (4:33 f.) or *bechire rashon*, "elect of [divine] good pleasure" (Manual of Discipline 8:6). Only he who has been touched by the elective grace of God and who has also accepted the divine offer of grace belongs to the elect of good pleasure, the *homines bonae voluntatis*. The lostness of the man who trusts only in himself and the meaning of divine providence is expressed with unusual clarity in a Qumrân hymn. In the Hymn Scroll 15:12–20 we read: "I have known in thy understanding that [a man's paths] are not in the hand of flesh and his way is not in man himself, nor can man [of himself] direct his steps. I have known also that in thy hand is the impulse of every man's spirit, [and all] his works thou didst determine before ever thou didst create him. How could anyone ever alter thy words? Only thou hast [created] the righteous and from the womb didst thou appoint him for the '*kairos* of good pleasure', to take heed to himself in thy covenant and to walk in all [that thou hast commanded], and [richly bestowed] mercy upon him in the abundance of thy grace, opening all the straitness of his soul to everlasting salvation and eternal peace when there is no want. Thou hast raised his dignity above the flesh. The wicked also hast thou created for the [last age] of thine [ang]er, and from the womb hast thou appointed them for the day of reckoning; for they walked in the way of the bad, spurned thy covenant, abhorred thy [truth], took no pleasure in that which thou hast commanded, and chose that which thou hatest. For acc[ording to the mysteries] of thy [understanding] thou hast determined to wreak a great judgment upon them".

There can be no doubt that here the deterministic view of human destiny is very far-reaching. The destiny of the righteous as well as of the sinners is already determined by God from the womb. Nevertheless, the sinners are punished for their wicked acts because they have wilfully separated themselves from the covenant of God and chosen what God hates. The good, on the other hand, who know that they belong to the congregation of the true covenant, belong to a penitential fellowship whose members "voluntarily declare themselves willing to turn away from all evil and adhere to all that he has commanded in his good pleasure" (Manual of Discipline 5:1), for which they are also rewarded by God. Hence this predestination by God does not eliminate reward and punishment. Thus the question still remains open whether the Qumrân Essenes believed in a doctrine of absolute predestination. If this was the case, it was by no means consistently thought out. One rather gains the impression that for them everything —including the acts of men—is determined in the knowledge of God, but that this still does not absolutely determine man, for he is able either to go on sinning or to repent. But he who has already abandoned sin and turned to God also knows that because of that act he belongs to those who have been chosen from the beginning to be the elect of divine good pleasure.

f) The Light-Darkness Doctrine, the Doctrine of the Two Spirits, and the Angelology of the Community

Closely connected with the question of divine providence

is the light-darkness doctrine of the community. God alone is responsible for the whole creation of the world. Thus we read in the hymn which concludes the Manual of Discipline 11:11: "Through his knowledge have all things come to be, and all that is he directs according to his plan. Without him nothing is done". But the creation itself is fulfilled in that the powers of light and darkness are both at work in it until the end of the world, for God "created the spirits of light and darkness and upon them he founded every work" (Manual of Discipline 3:25). These two spirits are at work also in man too "until the appointed time of his visitation" (Manual of Discipline 3:18; 4:19), and "according to each man's share of possession in the truth and righteousness he hates unrighteousness, and according to his inheritance in the lot of error he does wickedly and abhors the truth; for God has apportioned them [i.e., the spirits of error and of truth] in equal parts until the appointed end and [until] the new creation" (Manual of Discipline 4:24 f.). But when the "appointed time of the visitation" of God has come, he "will put an end to error and . . . destroy it for ever. Then will spring forth for all time the truth, which has wallowed in the ways of wickedness under the domination of error, [whose duration] is decreed until the appointed time of judgment" (Manual of Discipline 4:18–20). Thus the dualistic doctrine of the Qumrân Essenes has an eschatological character.

The powers of light and darkness are good and evil angels, which are led by a Prince of Light and an Angel of Darkness. Thus we read in the Manual of Discipline 3:20–24: "In the hand of the Prince of Light is dominion over all the sons of righteousness, [who therefore also] walk in the ways of light; and in the hand of the Angel of Darkness is all dominion over the sons of error, who [therefore also] walk in the ways of darkness. But the Angel of Darkness is also responsible for the straying of all the sons of righteousness, and all their sinfulness, their iniquities, their guilt, and their sinful works are under his dominion according to the secret counsel of God until the time of the end appointed by him. And all their [i.e., the sons of righteousness] afflictions and the appointed times of their distress are under the dominion of his 'temptation' and all the spirits of his lot [whose purpose it is] to make the sons of light stumble. But the God of Israel and the Angel of his truth help all the sons of light".

In the Qumrân texts the Prince of Light and the Angel of Darkness bear a number of names. In the passage cited they are also called "Angel of his truth" and *mastema*, a term designating personified temptation. In the War Scroll 13:10 we read that God appointed the Prince of Light from of old to help the sons of light, and in the War Scroll 17:6, it is apparently this angel who is called Michael. The evil power is simply called Belial. The age in which the community was formed is therefore called the "dominion of Belial" (e.g., Manual of Discipline 1:18), which will end with the victory of the power of light. Thus in the War Scroll 17:5 f. the Angel of Darkness is also called the "Prince of the Dominion of Wickedness".

In addition to these two leaders, the community recognized other angels who were subordinate to them. The Hymn Scroll 13:8 speaks of a "host of divine spirits" and 10:8 says of God, "Behold, thou art the prince of the godly, the king of the worthy, and the lord of every spirit". Here the terms "godly" and "worthy" clearly refer to angels. The Hymn Scroll uses still other phrases for the term "angel", such as, angel of the countenance, spirits of holiness, spirits of knowledge, sons of heaven, sons of God, heroes of power, heroes of the wonder, and warriors of heaven. The members of the community have fellowship with the good angels. Thus in the Hymn Scroll 3:21–3 we read: "I know that there is hope for him whom thou hast formed from the dust for the everlasting kingdom, and from great sin hast thou purified the perverse spirit to stand in his place with the host of the holy ones and to come into fellowship with the congregation of the sons of heaven. So thou hast cast for man an eternal lot with the spirits of knowledge to praise thy name together in joyful song and to recount thy wonders in the presence of all thy works". Hence, according to their view, the members of the sect participate in the heavenly liturgy, and therefore their services and their prayers were for them none other than a part of this liturgy. The members of the sect considered their relationship with the angels to be so close that, according to the Book of Rules 2:3–9, only Levitically pure persons could participate in the assemblies of the community, since "the angels of holiness are in their congregation".

This close connection between the community and the angels in the theology of the Qumrân Essenes also meant that for them, not only their community itself (cf. chap. IX,2,a), but also the angels participate in the eschatological event. Both are instruments of God's vengeance. Thus we read in the War Scroll 1:10 f., that on the day which God appointed of old for the final battle against the sons of darkness, "the congregation of the godly ones and the congregation of men will enter the battle together". Even more clearly the War Scroll 7:6 states that only Levitically pure men can participate in the final war "because the angels of holiness are with the hosts"; and in 12:7–9 a prayer praises God because he himself, along with his heavenly hosts, will help the community in the final battle. This battle of angels in the last days is also described in the Hymn Scroll 3:35 f.: "The host of heaven utter their voice and the pillars of the world tremble and shake. The war of the warriors of heaven spreads over the world and does not cease until the eternally appointed end. Nothing is like unto it!"

Very similar angelological concepts are found in the pseudepigrapha which belong in the Qumrân tradition. Thus in the Testament of Levi, chap. 3, for example, we read that in the second heaven are "all the spirits of retribution for vengeance on men", while the third heaven shelters "the hosts of the armies which are ordained for the day of judgment, to work vengeance on the spirits of deceit and of Belial". The fifth chapter of the Book of Jubilees and even more clearly the angelological part of the Book of Enoch attribute the sinfulness of the world to the evil spirits who will be annihilated with the help of the good angels at the last judgment. Enoch 6 deals with the fall of the evil angels, chapters 7 and 8 describe how they corrupt the earth, and in chapter 9, Michael, Uriel, Raphael, and Gabriel institute complaint before God concerning what has happened, pointing to God's all-embracing foreknowledge, for "thou knowest all things before they come to pass. Thou seest this and allowest it to happen. Thou tellest us not what we must do" (9:11). Chapter 10 describes how Uriel is entrusted with the announcement of the flood to Noah and how Raphael, Gabriel, and Michael are charged with the destruction of the fallen angels. Then follows still another eschatological vision. In chapter 15:8–12, the evil spirits are identified with the giants who were born of the union of fallen angels and the daughters of men (Gen. 6:24; Enoch 7:12; 15:3;

Jubilees 5:1) and 16:1 states that they will work corruption "until the day of the great last judgment when the world will come completely to an end for the watchers [i.e., angels] and the godless".

The brief reference of Josephus (*Bellum* 2,8,7) to the fact that the Essenes keep secret the names of the angels may also belong in this context.

g) *The Spirit in Man*

The word *ruach*, spirit, is often very difficult to translate in the Qumrân texts because sometimes it can mean the spirit in man, his mentality, his spiritual endowment, and at other times a spiritual power outside man which influences him, and again it may have both meanings at once. The Manual of Discipline 3:18 says that God gave to man "two spirits that he might walk by them until the appointed time of his visitation", and 4:23 declares that "thus far the spirits of truth and of error have been struggling in the heart of man". In the Hymn Scroll 15:13 *ruach* cannot be rendered otherwise than by "soul": "I know that in thy hand is the impulse of every soul". In the War Scroll 14:7 *ruach* means no more than mental willingness, the will. When the members of the sect here call themselves *'anwe ruach*, poor in spirit, they mean by this that they possess the willingness to be poor. When the term "spirits of knowledge" is used in the Hymn Scroll 3:22 and the term "spirit of knowledge" in the Manual of Discipline 3:18 f., what is meant is a human quality. In the Manual of Discipline 3:18 f. and 4:23 the "spirits of truth and of error" are mentioned and in the Manual of Discipline 4:21, "the spirit of truth" is described as a human, God-given quality. The spirits which are at work in the cosmos are thus also at work in man. But man is not only influenced by the spirits; his own spirit is subject to himself. There is an interrelation between them. This raises the same question which was posed in the section on providence and predestination (chap. VIII,3,e) as to how far divine influence upon men goes and what are the limits of the human will. Since man is in a certain respect himself a spiritual being, he is not completely subject to the spirits. He can also be called to account for whether he has given way to the good or the evil spirit in his soul. (Friedrich Nötscher, "Geist und Geister in den Texten von Qumrân", *Mélanges Bibliques rédigés en l'Honneur de André Robert*, 1957, pp. 305–15.)

h) *Knowledge, Secret Teachings,*
Gnosticism and Apocalypticism

In the Manual of Discipline 3:15 the whole creation is attributed to "the God of knowledge", who planned it even before the act of creation itself. But this order of creation is immanent in the fact of being and "nothing can be changed" (3:16). It is quite obvious that here, as later in Philo, particularly in the parable of the architect at the beginning of his work on the creation of the world, and also in a Haggadah in the Midrash Genesis Rabbah, par. 1, attributed to R. Hosha'ya the Great, the influence of Platonic-Stoic popular philosophy is at work. The divine order of creation is hidden from the ordinary sinful man, but he communicates it to those whom he has chosen for his covenant. This knowledge is the secret, arcane possession of the community; in the Hymn Scroll it is called *raze pele*'," marvellous mysteries". After praising God's act of creation, the author of Hymn Scroll 1:21 declares, "This I have known from thy understanding, for thou hast opened my ear for the marvellous mysteries".

By himself, man is utterly incapable of understanding these divine mysteries: "None can understand thy laws and none can gaze upon mysteries. For what is man—dust he is, of clay is he kneaded, and to dust he returns—that thou shouldst let him understand such wonderful things and know the mysteries of thy truth?" (Hymn Scroll, 10:2–5). Though the author of the Hymn Scroll can confidently assert: "Through me hast thou illumined the faces of many", he must nevertheless in the same breath humbly confess: "for thou didst permit me to know thy marvellous mysteries" (4:27).

The knowledge which has been bestowed upon the members of the community not only lifts them above other people but also unites them with the angels (cf. chap. VIII,3,f.). Thus we read in the Manual of Discipline 11:3–8: "For from the wellspring of his knowledge he has opened up my light and my eye has seen his wonderful works . . . and from the source of his righteousness [come] the precepts of light in my heart, through his marvellous mysteries my eye has gazed upon the eternal being: a saving knowledge which is hidden from the man of knowledge, a wise insight [which is hidden from] the sons of men, the wellspring of righteousness, the reservoir of strength, and the place of glory (*kavōd*). Of the company of flesh God gave this [knowledge] as an eternal possession to those whom he has chosen and allowed them to share in the lot of the holy ones, and with the sons of heaven he joined their fellowship to the council of the community". Here we find an even greater emphasis being put upon knowledge than is the case in the wisdom literature of the Old Testament. Knowledge in this sense means for the members of the Qumrân community a fact of salvation, inasmuch as nobody outside the group can share it.

Only the one whom God has illumined for his covenant is capable of such knowledge (Hymn Scroll 4:5).

To sum up, we may say, therefore, that the knowledge which is considered to be the salvatory possession of the community consists in knowing of God's work of creation and his providence and that the members of the sect who have this knowledge constitute, together with the angels, a community. Among other things, the subject of this knowledge is the dwelling-place of the glory (*kavōd*) of God. The sect was therefore familiar with esoteric doctrines which remind us strongly of similar teachings which appear later in the rabbinical literature. In the Mishnah, Hagigah II we read: "One dare not discuss incest laws in the presence of three, secrets of creation in the presence of two, and cosmic secrets of creation (*ma'aśeh merk'avah*) in the presence of a single person, except he be wise and knowing of his knowledge. . . . For him who does not have proper respect in the presence of the glory (*kavōd*) of his creator it would be better if he had never been born". A comparison of Tosephta Hagigah II,1 with Hagigah 14 b (bar) shows that the terms *kavōd* and *ma'aśeh merk'avah* can be used synonymously. The glory of the creator therefore means very much the same thing as "cosmic secrets of creation". In the passage cited from the Qumrân Hymn Scroll, which states that the members of the community gaze upon the wellspring of righteousness, the reservoir of strength, and the place of glory (*kavōd*), the meaning may well be similar.

The rabbinical mystics thought of the sphere of God's glory as being peopled by angels who repelled unqualified intruders. Thus in Hagigah 15 b we read: "The ministering angels were about to drive out even Rabbi Akiba. The Holy One, may he be praised, said to them: Let this

69

gray old man come in, for he is worthy to serve my glory (*kavōd*)". When the Qumrân people, who believed that they beheld the place of *kavōd*, thought of themselves as being in fellowship with the angels, a very similar conception may well have been responsible for this. The angelological portion of the Ethiopic Book of Enoch, which has especially close contact with the corresponding teachings of the Qumrân Essenes, contains in chapter 14 the account of Enoch's ascension, which can in many respects be regarded as a literary model for similar descriptions of ascensions which come from circles of rabbinical mystics of a later time (about the middle of the first century after Christ). The teaching concerning the pairs of opposites or syzygies in the Manual of Discipline (4:16,25) was also familiar to the later rabbinical mystics. The Manual of Discipline declares that men possess the potentiality for good and for evil in equal measure, and Hagigah 15 a states in a conversation between Acher and Rabbi Meir: "For everything the Holy One, praise be to him, created he also made a counterpart . . . he created the godly and the ungodly, he created paradise and hell. Everybody has two portions, one in paradise and one in hell. The godly man who has made himself deserving, receives his and his neighbour's portion in paradise; the godless man who has made himself guilty, receives his and his neighbour's portion in hell". The same conception is also found in a later Jewish mystical treatise, the Book of Jeshira (*circa* A.D. 500). It should be mentioned too that in Cave IV were also discovered fragments of an esoteric work and a heavenly liturgy which indicate connections with the Merkavah literature (cf. chap.I,3,a,ii).

It would thus appear to be irrefutable that the secret teachings must be related to the esoteric teachings found in rabbinical circles after the time of Johanan ben Zakkai, who was alive at the time of the destruction of the temple in the year A.D. 70; the only question that remains is whether both teachings should be described as Jewish Gnosticism. Such a designation would be justified only if it is possible to establish an historical and psychological connection between the religious-historical phenomenon of pagan and pagan-Christian gnosticism and this phenomenon of Jewish religious history. Otherwise it would be no more than a controversy over words and ideas. The Jewish esoteric teachings set out here do not operate in terms of a good transcendent God and an evil creator god, as did pagan Gnosticism; for the whole of creation, not merely the spirits of light but also the spirits of darkness, has at its source the one and only Creator-God. Nor are either the Qumrân texts or the rabbinical Merkavah speculations acquainted with the concept of a divine spark of light which must be liberated from the prison of the world, even though this idea is not entirely unknown in later cabbalistic teachings. Nevertheless, it seems to me that there is a very close connection between the Jewish esoteric teachings which we have cited and Gnosticism, not only because for both "knowledge" is a saving possession, and because the rabbinical Merkavah mystics spoke of the ascent of the soul through the seven heavens and thought of the heavenly world as being populated by evil angels, just as the pagan Gnostics thought of the *pleroma* as being inhabited by the archons, but also because both had a thoroughly negative attitude toward the present state of the world.

It has often been thought that there is a connection between Gnosticism and apocalypticism. The Qumrân texts have strengthened this theory. Both are expressions of a very similar attitude towards the world. The Gnostic, who despairs of the world, wants to get beyond the world into the sphere of divine transcendence; he desires as it were to flee from history, in which he can no longer find any meaning. The apocalyptist, on the other hand, holds to the revelation that the world was created good. He cannot make God solely responsible for his own shortcomings. His attitude towards the concrete world and concrete history, however, is like that of the Gnostic, except that through it all he remains bound to history and the world, both of which in their present form he wants to see abolished and recreated; he reaches out for the new world and the new aeon. Whereas the Gnostic wants to flee from the world, the apocalyptist seeks to get away from the present state of the world. Apocalypticism is thus the Jewish way out of the Gnostic temptation and therefore bears a very close relationship to Gnosticism. But the Qumrân texts show undeniably that the community lived in acute expectation of the last days (cf. chap. IX,2). In a series of apocalyptic writings, like the Apocalypse of Abraham, for example, which may, like the Qumrân texts, go back to an Essene source, as well as in the apocalypse in chapter 7 of the Book of Daniel, the view of the heavenly sphere is bound up with an eschatological insight into the divine plan of creation which extends to the end of the world. Moreover, the purpose of the apocalyptic revelation is in most cases an acutely eschatological one, even when it is not connected with an insight into the heavenly sphere. The light-darkness speculations of the Qumrân people themselves had such an eschatological point. This is particularly plain in a passage in the Manual of Discipline 4:18 f., on the two spirits and their operation in the world and in man: "But God in the secret counsel of his under

standing and in the wisdom of his glory will appoint an
end to perversity, and at the appointed time of visitation
he will destroy it for ever. Then the truth will spring forth
for all time on the earth". Thus eschatological expectation
and the tendency towards mystical speculation often go
hand in hand in Judaism. In this sense it is also noteworthy that it was sometimes the same Tannaitic rabbinical teachers to whom acute eschatological statements are
attributed who also concerned themselves with Merkavah
mysticism. Even Johanan ben Zakkai, whose acute-
messianic hopes were very slender if they existed at all,
nevertheless concerned himself with Merkavah mysticism,
and this mysticism was widespread especially in the circles
about Rabbi Akiba (cf. Hagigah 14 b) and therefore in a
generation whose acute messianic expectations led to the
Bar Kokhba revolt (A.D. 132–5). This knowledge of the
Merkavah sphere is related to various descriptions of
the end of the world and also to messianic calculations in
the later Hekaloth tractates, which date from the fourth
to the seventh century after Christ. Thus, for example, we
read in Hekalot rabbati 16:5 "When shall he see the
heavenly majesty? When shall he hear the last age of
redemption? When shall he see what no eye has yet seen?
When shall he rise up and make it known to the seed of
Abraham?"

Apocalypticism both as an insight into the divine sphere
and as an expression of acute eschatological thought is
therefore found in the writings of the broader field of
Essenism as well as later in those of the rabbinical circles.
When we remember that neither the apocalyptists nor the
Gnostics felt at home in the present world, that Gnosticism
as well as apocalypticism were concerned to give an answer
to the human questions thus raised, and that the Jewish

mystical speculations exhibit a number of motifs similar to those of pagan Gnosticism, we shall be compelled to characterize this Jewish mysticism, not only as Jewish heterodoxy, but also as Jewish Gnosticism. The more specific designation, Jewish Gnosticism, will adequately distinguish it from pagan Gnosticism, but the general term, Gnosticism, indicates the kinship of both phenomena in the history of religion. Thus one will not be wrong in seeing the germinal points of Jewish Gnosticism in many passages of the Qumrân Texts. It is of great significance in this connection that one of the Gnostic writings of Chenoboskion, the so-called "Tractate on the Three Natures", which gives a systematic exposition of Valentinian Gnosticism with an occidental complexion, contains statements concerning Jewish-Palestinian traditions, which are evidently taken from the Manual of Discipline of Qumrân. It is stated there that, according to these teachings, the work of God is twofold and is the source of good and evil, and that God brings about creation through his angels. With this we may compare the Manual of Discipline 3:25 "He created the spirits of light and of darkness, and upon them he founded every work".

It is true that no direct parallels to the phenomena just described can be drawn from the classical accounts of the Essenes, and yet they contain many references which can be understood in the sense we have indicated. Thus, for example, Philo reports in chapter 12 of his work, *Quod omnis probus liber sit*, that the Essenes do not concern themselves with formal logic but that they do cultivate that philosophical discipline which deals with the existence of God and the creation of the universe. Possibly the brief reference of Josephus in *Bellum* 2,8,7 to the fact that the Essenes kept secret the books of the sect and the names of the angels also belongs in this context. Another piece of information in *Bellum* 2,8,6 to the effect that they sought to learn from their writings about roots for banishing diseases and the properties of stones probably has no direct connection with these mystical, Gnostic teachings, but it does show that various secret doctrines were common in Essene circles. Josephus reports in *Ant.* 13,11,2; 15, 10,5; 17,13,3 that certain Essenes possessed the gift of prophecy and interpretation of dreams. This points towards the connections described above, since the members of the Qumrân community boast that they possess insight into the wonderful mysteries of God.

4. DIFFERENCES BETWEEN THE CLASSICAL ACCOUNTS OF ESSENISM AND THE QUMRÂN TEXTS

In the introduction to this chapter we pointed out a number of differences which may be largely explained by the fact that Philo and Josephus were writing for Hellenistic readers, for whom some teachings had to be made palatable and others even withheld. It is generally known that Philo especially—in his other writings also—took this course by making use of the allegorical method. The work of Josephus also has an apologetic character and consequently in his description of Essenism he was obliged to suppress all those aspects which would have an unfavourable effect upon Greeks and Romans. We shall therefore have to give up once and for all the habit of seeing the Essenes through the Hellenizing spectacles of these two writers and of taking these two descriptions as a standard and norm in other respects simply because they contain a great deal which is correct. Thus in Philo and Josephus the teachings concerning the covenant theology and the

75

last days are almost completely lacking or are subjected to severe reinterpretation. We can therefore safely amplify the accounts of Philo and Josephus with the Qumrân material in all those details in which these writers, from their point of view, had good reason to be silent. But where there are still other discrepancies—especially in regard to organizational and cultic details—they require the most thorough investigation and careful study.

Among the first peculiarities of the Qumrân texts to be noted is the Teacher of Righteousness, mentioned in several manuscripts, who to all appearances was not the founder of all the Essene communities, but may probably have founded the Qumrân group (cf. chap. VIII). In his time, as the Habakkuk Commentary indicates, the messianic expectation of the last days was at its height and the community hoped for an eschatological war of vengeance upon the enemies of God, who in their opinion included not only the sinful Israelites but also all the heathen (cf. chap. IX,2,2). The appearance of the Teacher of Righteousness resulted in an even greater increase in these hopes and feelings. How could Josephus Flavius or Philo have included such a personality in their presentation without completely contradicting the aim of their writings? Also in this category is Philo's account in *Quod omnis probus liber sit*, chap. 12, in which he reports that the Essenes were perfectly peaceable people and that they never manufactured any kinds of weapons or shields. On the basis of the Qumrân texts, and especially the War Scroll. this report must be called inconclusive and false.

In *Bellum* 2,8,5, Josephus says of the Essenes: "In an extraordinary way they reverence the divinity. Before the sun rises they speak not a single profane word but instead address to the stars certain ancient prayers, as if they made supplication for its rising". Even though the construction of this account betrays a Hellenistic manner of speech, it does nevertheless refer fairly clearly to a kind of veneration of the sun. It is true that the texts so far discovered furnish no direct parallels to this account, and yet it appears very probable that there was a high regard for the sun in the circles of the Qumrân Essenes. In contrast with the rest of Judaism, the Qumrân Essenes counted the years according to a solar calendar (cf. chap. VIII,3,d). In the large cemetery to the east of Qumrân the bodies were all buried in a north-south position, that is with the head in the direction of the sun. It would appear that here, too, Josephus' account is based upon a good tradition.

In *Bellum* 2,8,7,9 it is stated that even as a postulant the Essene received from the order a loin cloth, a white garment, and a small hatchet for the burying of excrement. There is nothing whatsoever in the Qumrân texts with which to compare this account. According to Philo in *Quod omnis probus liber sit*, chap. 12, the Essenes also worked outside the community in civil vocations and handed over their wages to the common treasury. This account has not yet been confirmed by the Qumrân texts either. Though the Manual of Discipline speaks very clearly of a common treasury (cf. chap. VIII,2,a), earning wages outside the community itself does not seem very probable on the basis of the regulations of the Sectarian Canon. It is possible that in this instance Philo had in mind an Essene group other than the Qumrân Essenes.

With regard to the extent and range of Essenism and the groups which possibly existed within its framework, we are still inadequately informed, despite the discovery of the Qumrân texts. The relationship between Essenism and other Jewish groups, such as the movement of John the Baptist and the Zealots has, it is true, become much clearer than before, but even so in this area we are still thrown back upon conjectures and probabilities. The unanimous report of Philo and Josephus (*Quod omnis probus liber sit*, chap. 12 and *Ant.* 18,1,5) that there were over four thousand Essenes falls within this category too. It would appear that both reports referred to the monastic Essenes only and not to the married members of the Essene groups. As far as the Essene colonies are concerned, there are conflicting accounts even among the classical writers. Pliny (*Naturalis Historia* 5:15) speaks of a monastic Essene settlement on the west side of the Dead Sea. He may have had Qumrân in mind. Philo's account actually contradicts itself. In the passage cited above, he says that the Essenes lived in villages and avoided cities because of the sinfulness of their inhabitants; and in his "Apology for the Jews" (fragments preserved in Eusebius, *Praeparatio Evangelica*, 8:11) he says: "They dwell in many cities of Judea and in many villages, and constitute large and populous communities". This last account coincides with Josephus' statement in *Bellum* 2,8,4: "They have no one certain city, but many of them dwell in every city". The Damascus Document (7:6a f.) also presupposes a number of colonies of the community—speaking here in express terms of married members of the community: "If they dwell in camps according to the order of the land which has been maintained from of old, and take wives according to the custom of the Torah and beget children, they shall conduct themselves according to the law". In the same way, the Manual of Discipline 6:2 speaks of "all their dwellings", which, as the context indicates apparently means monastic settlements. Hence we see that, because of many things which still remain unclear to-day, there are still numerous problems to be solved in the history of the development of Essenism, notwithstanding the Qumrân texts. Some of the questions which are still outstanding will doubtless be answered once all the texts from the caves of Qumrân are published.

IX

THE COMMUNITY THEOLOGY AND THE ESCHATOLOGICAL EXPECTATION OF THE QUMRÂN ESSENES

I. THE COVENANT THEOLOGY

a) Covenant and Election

FOLLOWING the teaching of the Old Testament prophets, the Qumrân community regarded itself as the elect *remnant* of Israel which would emerge in the last days from the purging judgment of God. The theology of the remnant held by the community is briefly summarized in the Damascus Document 2:14 – 3:20. First, it says, the angels fell because of their rebellious thoughts (cf. chap. VIII,3,f) and begat sons who were as tall as cedars and large as mountains. Thereupon all men on earth died. Even the sons of Noah fell victim to sin, but not Abraham, Isaac and Jacob. These were therefore accepted as friends of God and partners in his everlasting covenant. The sons of Jacob, however, sinned again in Egypt and for this they were punished during the wanderings in the wilderness. Thus "the first that entered the covenant" were punished and delivered up unto the sword, "because they forsook the covenant of God, performed their own will, and allowed themselves to be led astray by their rebellious thoughts. Among those, however, who were left, who had held fast to God's commandments, God established his covenant with Israel forever". Concerning this choosing of the final remnant, the Damascus Document 1:4–10 says, "When God remembered the covenant with the first ones, he left a remnant of Israel which he did not give up to destruction. And in the last age of wrath, three hundred and ninety years (cf. Ezek. 4:5), after he had given them into the hand of Nebuchadnezzar, king of Babylon, he visited them and there sprouted forth from Israel and from Aaron (cf. chap. VII) the root of a plant to take possession of his land and to thrive in his good soil. Then they perceived their iniquity and knew that they were guilty men. For twenty years they were as blind men, groping their way. Then God recognized their works, for with pure hearts they had sought him, and so raised up for them the Teacher of Righteousness to lead them in the way of his heart". Thus from the beginning right to the End—in which the community believed it was living—God saves for himself a chosen remnant (Dam. Doc. 2:11). In the War Scroll 13:8 the conviction is expressed that God will grant help to this chosen remnant in the struggle of the last days. The chastisements of God come upon the people only so that through them the remnant may be purified. In the face of the general sinfulness the author of the Hymn Scroll 6:7 f. recognizes the smallness of the band of the elect; "for I have known that thou dost raise to life only a small portion of thy people and a remnant of thine inheritance".

As a counterpart to this view of the remnant, the texts declare that the wicked and the transgressors will have no remnant that will survive the appointed time of God's visitation. According to the Manual of Discipline 4:14, the fate of the evil and the evil spirits is to perish "without any remnant". The same fate is prophesied for them in the Damascus Document 2:6 f.

Again, following an Old Testament image, Isaiah. 60:21,

the community compared itself with the root or the shoot of a *planting*, which is set into the ground as a small, tender plant, but will grow up into a magnificent tree. We have already mentioned the passage in the Damascus Document, 1:7, which speaks of the root, the plant which blossomed out of Israel and Aaron. The Manual of Discipline 8:4–6 says even more clearly, "When these things come to pass in Israel, the council of the community will be established in the truth for an eternal planting, a sanctuary for Israel and a holy of holies for Aaron". In the Hymn Scroll 6:15; 8:6,10 the terms "an eternal planting" and "the planting of the truth" occur together. Likewise, in the Ethiopic Book of Enoch 10:16, at the beginning of a description of the messianic glory, we read: "There shall appear the plant of righteousness and truth". And again according to Enoch 93:10 (Apocalypse of the Ten Weeks), "the chosen righteous of the eternal planting of righteousness" are to be selected at the end of the seventh week.

Although the community regarded itself only as a remnant of a much larger *massa damnata*, it was believed that this small, insignificant remnant was the sole scion that would inherit the promises of Israel. Anybody who did not belong to the remnant was actually no longer a member of the chosen people of Israel. The violators of the covenant (Dan. 11:32) unite with the sinful heathen and therefore, according to the War Scroll 1,1 f., are to be counted among the sons of darkness. The community which was made up of the sons of light, which was the planting of righteousness and truth and the chosen remnant, therefore regarded itself as the eschatological whole of Israel. So we are not surprised to read in the first lines of the Book of Rules: "This is the rule for the whole congregation of Israel in the last days".

This is the sense in which the *covenant theology* of the community is also to be understood. The covenant made with the patriarchs is indissoluble. According to the Damascus Document 3:4, Abraham, Isaac, and Jacob are covenant partners for ever. Because the majority of the people always leaned towards sin, however, and only a small remnant was able to withstand temptations, the covenant had also to be renewed with the remnant. The Old Testament origin of this conception was provided for the Qumrân people by Jeremiah 31:31, where it is said that in the last days God will make a new covenant with Israel which cannot ever again be broken. The author of the Habakkuk Commentary 2:3 thought of this renewed covenant as having already come, for the apostates from the new covenant are accused of not having believed in the covenant of God. The same conception occurs also in the Damascus Document 20:12, which says of the followers of the Man of the Lie "that they rejected the covenant of God and the pledge which they established in the land of Damascus, that is, the new covenant". The question whether the land of Damascus is Damascus in the geographical or merely in a figurative sense cannot be decided at this point. In any case, it is certain that it refers to an exodus of the community from sinful Jerusalem. But whether Damascus is perhaps to be understood merely as an alternative name for Qumrân or similar places, as some think, is immaterial. The covenant that was there renewed is, according to the Manual of Discipline 4:22, an eternal covenant. He who belongs to this covenant knows that God has elected him, for the man who stands by himself alone would not be capable of being faithful to the covenant. Thus we read in the Hymn Scroll 2:28: "When my heart dissolves like water, thou strengthenest my soul in thy covenant", and in 7:19 f. the author gives thanks to God, "for thy righteousness hast thou appointed me for thy covenant". The conception of the new covenant among the Qumrân Essenes thus comes close to that of the New Testament writings, but does not reach it, a point which will be discussed later (cf. chap. XI,3).

The community's and the individual members' *conviction of election* also belongs in this context. In the community, according to the Manual of Discipline 1,4, are "all whom God has chosen". In 8:6 they are called the "elect of [divine] favour" and in 9:14 "the elect of time". In the Hymn Scroll 4:33 f. the members also call themselves "sons of his favour". As such they have insight into the divine mysteries (Manual of Discipline 11:7; cf. chap. VIII,3,h) and their task is to wage the eschatological war of vengeance against the heathen nations (Hab. Com. 5:4; cf. chap. IX,2,a). The Hymn Scroll lays greater stress upon the individual election of the individual members of the community than upon the election of the community as a whole. The reason for this lies in the literary structure of the Hymn Scroll, since its theme is the destiny of the individual man. Thus the author says of himself in 2:13: "Thou liftest me up as a banner for the elect of righteousness and as a proclaimer of knowledge in the wonderful mysteries"; and in 15:23: "I desired to enter the congregation of thy holiness, because I knew that thou hast chosen it from all and that it will serve thee for ever"; for thou art just and thine elect are truth" (14:15). The chosen remnant regarded itself as a fellowship of penitents, "who declared their willingness to turn away from all evil and hold fast to all that he in his good pleasure has commanded" (Manual of Discipline 5:1).

b) Poverty as a Sign of Faithfulness to the Covenant

In the Qumrân texts, as is also frequently the case in the post-exilic Old Testament literature, poverty signifies not merely a social condition, but furthermore a religious concept. According to the theology of the community, unchastity and desire for worldly riches are *the* sins, and are the sins which are the cause of all other sins. Through money, Belial, the devil, gains possession of man; the rich man who gathers wealth and is concerned about his goods thereby opens the door of his soul to the devil. The saying, "You cannot serve God and mammon" (Luke 16:13; Matt. 6:24), might well have appeared in every one of the Dead Sea texts, for mammon is the instrument and weapon of the devil. Thus in the Manual of Discipline 10:19, the author says in his prayer, "For sinful wealth I have no desire", and in the Hymn Scroll 15:23, "I have come to know that no wealth can equal thy truth". Concerning the sinners, Dam. Doc. 8,5 says that they "wallowed in the ways of lewdness and in the wealth of wickedness." Though the individual can be defiled and led into sin through riches, yet property in itself is not sinful, for even the community itself has control of the commonly administered property (cf. chap. VIII,2,a), and in the Habakkuk Commentary 12:9 f., the wicked priest is denounced for having plundered the "property of the poor" in the cities of Judea. The Manual of Discipline 9:8 also speaks of "the property of the men of holiness", which, according to 9:7, is to be administered by Aaronite priests. The actual officer who took over the property of the novices when they were received into the order bore the title of an overseer of the work of the full members (6:20). Moreover, the still unpublished copper scroll is said to contain

85

information relating to buried treasures. The property of the community came into being through the fact that the newly-admitted, at least as far as the monastic group was concerned, were required to surrender their private property (Manual of Discipline 1:11 f.). But all property which was not put at the disposal of the community was regarded as unclean, for "the property of the men of holiness, who walk blamelessly, dare not be combined with the property of the men of deceit". (9:8).

The poverty of the members of the sect, or even better, their readiness to accept poverty, was regarded by them as a state of grace by which they could identify themselves with the pious and the elect. In the Hymn Scroll 2:31 f. even the author identifies himself with the poor: "I praise thee, O Lord, for thine eye rests upon me and thou deliverest me from the avidity of the preacher of lies; from the congregation of hypocrites hast thou freed the poor, whose blood they destroy, shedding it for thy service". The poor man therefore belongs to the congregation of the elect; his readiness to accept poverty is a charismatic gift, and accordingly the Hymn Scroll 5:22 also speaks of the *ebyone chesed*, the "poor of grace", the poor by grace. The Dead Sea sect was not a proletarian movement which promised those who did not prosper on this earth a heavenly compensation for their earthly poverty, but rather demanded a person's acceptance of poverty, even though from a purely external point of view he was well-to-do, which might well have been the case of those members of the community who, according to the Damascus Document (7:6 af.; 14:12–14), were married and had to surrender only two days' earnings monthly to the communal fund for social purposes. In the monastic community the requirement for poverty went so far that the individual members surrendered their property to a common treasury and practised community of goods. In consequence of this readiness to accept poverty, the members of the community also called themselves, in the War Scroll 14:7, *'anwe ruach*, "the poor in spirit", the poor in will, that is, the poor by their own consent, those who are ready to accept the state of poverty. Here again the parallels with the New Testament are especially striking, but we shall discuss this in more detail in another context (cf. chap. XI,2,c).

This charismatic poverty was a part of their eschatological thinking. Already in Isaiah 61:1–2 we read that the messianic liberation is to be proclaimed to the poor: "The Spirit of the Lord God is upon me, because the Lord has anointed me to bring good tidings to the poor; he has sent me to bind up the brokenhearted, to proclaim liberty to the captives, and the opening of the prison to those who are bound; to proclaim the year of the Lord's favour, and the day of vengeance of our God; to comfort all who mourn". As the Hymn Scroll 18:14 indicates, this passage from Isaiah was employed theologically by the Qumrân people. The people of Nazareth broke out into messianic enthusiasm when they heard these words from the lips of Jesus (Luke 4:18 ff.), and Jesus himself is recorded as having quoted them when he was questioned about his messiahship by the disciples of John (Matt. 11:5; Luke 7:22). The same meaning is found in a prayer in the War Scroll 11:7–9: "By thine anointed ones, the seers of testimonies, thou hast made known to us the last times of the wars of thy hands, to prove thyself in power against our enemies, to make the troops of Belial fall, the seven vain nations, by the poor of thy redemption". And similarly we read in 11:13: "Into the hands of the poor wilt thou deliver the enemies of all lands", and in 13:14: "The hand of thy strength is with the poor". Thus the poor are not merely passively the redeemed of God; they also have the active task of waging God's eschatological war of vengeance (cf. chap. IX,2,a).

Thus, those who belonged to the community felt themselves to be the poor in the sense we have described. On the other hand, the question whether the members of the sect described themselves before the world as poor, and whether one may look upon the term "poor men" as a name which the community gave itself, is secondary. This is not stated explicitly in the passages cited and yet the term *ebyonim* in the Habakkuk Commentary 12:3.6.10 could be a designation of the community. The Commentary on Psalm 37 from Cave IV, 2:10, speaks even more clearly of a "congregation of the poor". Therefore we may very possibly be justified in looking upon the term "the poor" as one of the numerous self-descriptions of the community. And thus it also seems very probable that the name of the Jewish Christian sect of the Ebionites, which was also strongly influenced by Essene views, was derived from the Qumrân Essenes' designation *ebyonim*.

2. THE ESCHATOLOGICAL EXPECTATIONS

a) *The Eschatological War of Vengeance*

The community of Qumrân was preparing itself for an eschatological war of vengeance upon its enemies and the enemies of God. This war which was to take place in the last days is described not only in the War Scroll, which is devoted especially to this theme, but is also referred to more or less explicitly in almost all the other texts. In the community of Qumrân, which believed that it was itself living in the last days (cf. chap. IX,2,c), nothing happened which was without an eschatological purpose. Because they regarded themselves as the elect eschatological remnant of Israel, its members lived a strictly ascetic life and cherished a charismatic ideal of poverty. But for this reason they also considered themselves to be the chosen host, which along with the angels (cf. chap. VIII,3,f.) would wage the final war against the evil ones, the servants of Belial. The community was incapable of distinguishing between the Evil One and the evil ones; for them they were identical. Thus the Manual of Discipline 8:6 f. states that "it is the [task] of the elect of [divine] favour to make atonement for the earth and requite the wicked". This idea is even more clearly expressed in the Habakkuk Commentary 5:3,: "This means that God will not utterly exterminate his people by the hand of the heathen nations, but by the hand of his elect will God execute judgment upon all heathen nations; and when these are chastized all the wicked among his own people will also be punished". The passage at the beginning of the War Scroll, 1:1 f. says, precisely the same thing: "This is the book of the rules of the war; At the beginning is the battle of the sons of light, to begin it against the lot of the sons of darkness, against the army of Belial, against the troop of Edom, Moab, and the sons of Ammon, and against the host of the dwellers in Philistia and the troops of the Kittim of Assyria—and together with them are the violators of the covenant". In their description of the eschatological vengeance to be wreaked upon the enemies of the righteous elect the exhortations of Enoch are expressed in unusually trenchant terms. According to Enoch 91:12, the "sinners shall be delivered into the hands of the righteous". And in Enoch 95:3–7 we read: "Fear not the sinners, ye righteous; for again will the Lord deliver them into your hands, that ye may execute judgment upon them according to your desires. . . . Woe to you who requite your neighbour with evil; for ye shall be requited according to your works. . . . Woe to you, sinners for ye persecute the righteous; for ye shall be delivered up and persecuted because of injustice, and heavy shall be their [i.e., the righteous'] yoke upon you". And Enoch 96:1: "Be hopeful, ye righteous; for suddenly shall the sinners perish before you, and ye shall have lordship over them according to your desires". Enoch 98:12: "Woe to you who love the deeds of unrighteousness: wherefore do ye hope for good hap unto yourselves? know that ye shall be delivered into the hands of the righteous, and they shall cut off your necks and slay you, and have no mercy upon you". Similarly we read in Jubilees 23:30: "And at that time the Lord will heal his servants, and they shall rise up and see great peace, and drive out their adversaries. And the righteous shall see all their judgments and all their curses on their enemies".

This militant eschatological spirit is probably most clearly expressed in the prayer before battle which the priest addresses to the soldiers: "Arise, O warrior; lead away thy prisoners; man of power, seize thy plunder; thou who dost valiantly, lay thy hand on the necks of thy enemies and set thy foot on the heaps of the slain. Smite the nations, thy adversaries, and let thy sword consume the guilty flesh. Fill thy land with glory and thy inheritance with blessing. May there be much cattle in thy fields, silver, gold, and precious stones in thy palaces. Zion, rejoice exceedingly, shine forth with songs of joy, O Jerusalem, and exult, all ye cities of Judah! Keep open thy gate continually, that the might of nations may be brought into thee. Their kings will minister to thee and all thy oppressors will lie in dust before thee" (War Scroll 12:10–14).

According to the War Scroll 1:3, the eschatological war will begin "when the exiled sons of light return from the wilderness of the nations to encamp in the wilderness of Jerusalem". Like the *Hasidim rishonim*, the Qumrân Essenes, basing their thought upon Isaiah 40:3, regarded the wilderness as the place of salvation from which the messianic event will begin (cf. chap. VI,2). In other words, the war of the sons of light against the sons of darkness will take place at the beginning of the messianic era. It would last for forty years (2:8–14; cf. chap. IX,2,d). During this period of time there will be no fighting in every seventh year, that is, every sabbath year. However, according to the War Scroll, the enemies also will not venture a counter-attack in these years, but will apparently be glad that they themselves are not being attacked. The final war will be accomplished completely according to plan; the decree of God, whose instrument the Qumrân community believed itself to be, cannot be stayed by anything. The thirty-five years of actual war are subdivided into four periods. During the first six years of war up to the first sabbath year the whole congregation will fight together, since it will be necessary to clear the holy land of enemies. During the next nine years, only a number of armies will continue the fight against more distant foes. During the two remaining periods of ten years each, certain armies will fight and conquer the sons of Ham and the sons of Japheth. The course of the war, the disposition of the troops, the trumpet corps, and the equipment of the sons of light are described in detail in the War Scroll. The enemies are given no active part whatsoever; indeed, they are described right from the beginning as the "fallen".

The final war therefore has such a schematic character that it gives the effect of being unreal. This impression, however, is intentional on the part of the author of the War Scroll. The real greatness of God only becomes clear and apparent to all if those powers, which now determine the course of history, are reduced at the end of the world to completely impotent, purely passive entities. In this last battle the angels of God join with the sons of light as a decisive factor (cf. chap. VIII,3,f.). And yet before this there will be battles which God will not influence. In these battles the sons of light will win three times and the hosts of Belial will be the victor three times, but "the seventh time the strong hand of God will overthrow Belial, and all the angels of his dominion and all the men of his lot will be exterminated for ever" (1:13–15). This is when, as the texts quoted above clearly indicate, God will give to the congregation of the poor, of his redemption, that power over his and their enemies (cf. chap. IX,1,b), for which the Qumrân people were waiting so eagerly. A general, eschatologically-determined hatred of enemies was therefore propagated among the Qumrân Essenes.

It is in this connection too that we must understand Josephus' brief note in *Bellum* 2,20,4, which states that in the Jewish-Roman war (A.D. 66–70) an Essene named John was entrusted with the command of the strategically very important triangle of Lydda, Jaffa, and Emmaus, which controlled communications between Jerusalem and the sea coast. Hippolytus (*Adv. Haer.* 10,26) also speaks of a Zealotist branch of the Essenes, although his account, even though it may be based upon good sources, has a strong legendary character.

It is possible, therefore, through this militant expectation of the last days, to prove all those accounts of the

Essenes to be unhistorical which speak of them as peaceful men who had rejected the manufacture and use of instruments of war (cf. chap. VIII,4). On the other hand, however, certain relationships of ideas between Essenism and Zealotism are rendered probable, though the present state of research does not permit any more precise statements with regard to them.

b) The Kittim

In the last days, according to the expectation of the Qumrân community, there will arise an evil heathen nation which will attack the people of Israel as a sign of God's wrath and a scourge of God, but which in the end will be conquered with all the other godless by the sons of light. The author of the Habakkuk Commentary, 2,10–13, applies the verse Hab. 1:6, "For lo, I am rousing the Chaldeans, that bitter and hasty nation", to this proud nation of the last days in the following way: "This means the Kittim, who are swift and strong in war and have the strength to destroy many". According to 9:4–7, in the last days they will confiscate all the wealth which the last priests of Jerusalem have assembled. They are described in detail in the Habakkuk Commentary, Columns 3, 4 and 6. They smite and plunder the cities; dread and terror of them oppresses all the nations; their horses and their animals—war elephants or transport—trample the earth; they mock at kings and princes and scoff at great armies. Their rulers overthrow the fortresses of the peoples with ease. In this way they constantly increase their wealth, which means, in the author's opinion, that, since wealth is an instrument of the devil (cf. chap. IX,1,b), they are constantly contributing to their own final eschatological downfall. Their wealth does not come only from their plunderings, but all the peoples are forced to pay tribute to them year by year. In their campaigns they are very cruel; they kill youths, men and old men, women and little children with the sword, and even on the unborn they have no mercy. So much for the general statements; but the Habakkuk Commentary also contains more specific statements concerning the Kittim. According to 3:11, they come from far away, from the islands of the sea. In 4:10–12 it is said of their rulers that "in the council of their 'house of sin' one passes one before the other, and one after another rules". In 6:3–5 there is a clear reference to a cult of war standards among the Kittim: "The interpretation is that they sacrifice to their standards and their weapons of war are for them the object of cultic veneration".

But their power, too, is limited, like everything else that is subject to the laws of this world and is ruled and determined by Belial. When God "at the appointed time of his visitation" (Manual of Discipline 3:18; 4:18) exterminates the evil for ever (cf. chap. VIII,3,f) and breaks the power of the devil, the glory of the Kittim will also cease. And since the sons of light will, according to their own eschatological conception, play an active role in the eschatological drama (cf. chap. IX,2,a), the destruction of the Kittim will also devolve upon them. According to the War Scroll 1:2, they will advance against, among others, "the Kittim of Assyria", with whom the violators of the covenant are allied. Thus in 15:2 f., we read: "And all the warriors shall go and pitch camp against the king of the Kittim and against all the army of Belial that are predestined with him for the day of vengeance by God's sword".

And here the question, which was much debated among the specialists in connection with the dating of the Habakkuk Commentary, arises as to whom the Kittim really were, what historical nation provided the model for the term. This much-discussed problem, however, cannot be answered so absolutely and in such a hard and fast way that one interpretation completely rules out the possibility of the correctness of another. There are really only two peoples who enter into the picture, Greeks (i.e. Diadochian states) and Romans. All other peoples to the south and east of Palestine are out of the question, because already in the old Testament the Kittim represented the extreme west (Jer. 2:10) and also because, according to the Habakkuk Commentary, they are said to come "from far away, from the islands of the sea". The islands of the Kittim are mentioned not only in Jer. 2:10 but also in Ezek. 27:6, where they are referred to as suppliers of timber for shipbuilding. The general description of the Kittim in the Habakkuk Commentary points to a wicked people of the last days who show no mercy. They even go so far as to make sacrifices to their battle standards. Now, we have evidence of a cult of battle standards in the Roman armies in the time of the empire and therefore many have concluded that the Kittim were the Romans. And yet there are sources which would make it appear that the use of the term as applied to the Seleucid kings is not altogether precluded. Those who argue that the Kittim are the Seleucids of the period of the Maccabean struggles interpret their animals, which trample the earth, as meaning war elephants; but this argument too is not convincing, since the Hebrew language has its own word for "elephant". On the other hand, however, the author's predilection for pseudonyms and circumlocutions might have gone so far as to cause him to use the word "animals" for "elephants". Another starting-point for extensive controversies is the reference in the Habakkuk Commentary to the fact that the rulers of the Kittim discharge their duties one after another. This has been thought to be a reference to the Roman provincial governors who succeeded one another or to the Seleucid dynasty, which was so completely disorganized because of confusion in the line of succession that kings and anti-kings were constantly replacing one another. The term "house of sin" used in this connection has accordingly been regarded as a description of the Roman senate or the Seleucid dynasty. The references in the Habakkuk Commentary are therefore so general that it is impossible to draw any conclusion regarding the time when the commentary was written, simply because the Kittim cannot with certainty be identified either with the Seleucids or with the Romans. They are *the* evil people of the last days, and the Seleucids as well as the Romans contributed to the external picture we get from the description. An important point for the dating of the commentary is the statement that in the last days the Kittim will confiscate the wealth of the priests of Jerusalem, which probably means that at the time of writing they had not yet come into power in Palestine. The date of the Habakkuk Commentary will therefore have to be set in a period when the Seleucids were no longer ruling and the Romans were not yet in power in Palestine. Thus the year 63 B.C. is the *terminus antequem*.

Nor do the Old Testament references and the remaining references to the Kittim in the Qumrân literature bring us nearer a solution. In Gen. 10:4 and I Chron. 1:7 they are called sons of Javan, and thus belong to the Greeks (Javan = Ionia). According to Isa. 23:1,12, they had trade relations with Tyre, and in Jer. 2:10 and Ezek. 27:6 the islands of the Kittim are mentioned. In I Macc. 1:1 and 8:5 the Greeks are described by the name of Kittim. Alexander the Great, who came out of the land of the Kittim, had been king in Greece before he conquered Darius, king of the Persians, and became "the great king" in his stead. Again in Dan. 11:30 the term Kittim signifies the Romans. Thus precisely in the literature of the time which relates to the Qumrân texts the term Kittim refers to both Greeks and Romans. Hence it is very possible that the position may be similar in the Qumrân texts themselves. Therefore our method must be not to try to understand the described historical circumstances on the basis of the term, but to start the opposite way round and try to define the term "Kittim" by understanding the historical allusions. But since the historical allusions are also very ambiguous, it would appear to be almost hopeless to find a more accurate definition of the Kittim.

Those who would identify the Kittim with the Greeks find their view borne out in the War Scroll 1:2 where the Kittim of Assyria are mentioned ând in 1:4, where the Kittim of Egypt are mentioned. It is true that it is natural to think of the Seleucids and Ptolemies, but such an interpretation is not necessarily correct. In 1:4, immediately before the reference to the Kittim, there is a gap in the text whose contents cannot be supplied with certainty, and, besides, this passage is not speaking of the Kittim of Egypt, but only of the Kittim *in* Egypt. It is therefore very possible that nothing is being said here beyond the fact that the Kittim in Egypt and the Kittim of Assyria are ethnographically related. But this interpretation, too, leaves the two possible arguments in favour of Greeks and Romans open, for from the point of view of common Greek culture and common Greek origin, the Seleucids and the Ptolemies can be called Kittim just as correctly as one can say that the Romans in Syria and in Egypt are everywhere the same, namely, Romans. Somewhat more illuminating is a statement in the Nahum Commentary from Cave IV, which reads: "the kings of Javan (i.e., Greece) from Antiochus until the accession of the rulers of the Kittim" (1:3). The Antiochus mentioned means either Antiochus the Great, III (223–187 B.C.) or, more probably, Antiochus IV (175–164 B.C.). The time is reckoned from him, who is called a king of Greece, to the accession of the rulers of the Kittim. Thus in this passage, in contrast to I Macc. 1:1, the meaning may be the Kittim as distinct from the Greeks, which would probably mean that here they are to be identified with the Romans. The meaning of this passage, however, gives no clue to the interpretation of the Kittim in the other scrolls. Nor does the derivation of the name "Kittim" tell us anything more than that they came from the west. In all probability it derives from the name of the city of Kition on the southern coast of Cyprus.

The idea of a struggle against a wicked hostile power in the last days is familiar to us in the Old Testament. In Ezek. 38:1–39:29, Gog of the land of Magog personifies this ultimate hostile army. Joel 3:9–10, reversing the figure of the peaceful kingdom (Isa. 2:4; Mic. 4:3), states it with unusual clarity:

"Proclaim this among the nations:
Prepare war, stir up the mighty men.
Let all the men of war draw near, let them come up.
Beat your plowshares into swords, and your pruning
hooks into speaks; let the weak say, 'I am a warrior' ".

c) *The Last Days and the Last Age of Wickedness*

The Qumrân Essenes, like their predecessors, the *Hasidim rishonim*, lived in eager expectation of the last days (cf.

chap. VII). The term *'aharit ha-jamim*, "end of days", like the terms "coming world" and "future", later documented in the rabbinical literature, therefore has no one comprehensive meaning. On the one hand, it signifies the last days of this world in the broad sense and on the other, the actual final period with its wars, followed by the time of salvation. Consequently, the meaning of the term can only be inferred from the context, and its meaning may also vary within one and the same text. The Habakkuk Commentary 2:5-9 uses the term in the first sense when it speaks of the apostates of the last days who are not willing to accept the eschatological message of the priestly Teacher of Righteousness. These apostates are manifestly contemporaries of the author. But yet he also speaks of the last days as something in the future. In 9:6 we read that in the last days the wealth of the last priests of Jerusalem will be given over to the armies of the Kittim. In the first sense the Qumrân community also regards itself as the Israel of the last days (Book of Rules 1:1).

There is no doubt that the Qumrân community had to suffer many a disappointment in its eschatological expectation in the course of its history. Already the expectation of an imminent end, cherished by the *Hasidim*, had been disappointed (cf. chap. VII). The year 164 B.C. did bring a restoration of the cultus, but it was far from being the messianic event. In the apocalypse of the Seventy Shepherds and the apocalypse of the Ten Weeks in the Book of Enoch (90; 93; 91: 12-17), which can be dated soon after this time, the actual last age likewise follows upon only a brief period of pre-messianic confusion. In the apocalypse of the Ten Weeks, the end of the sixth week is dated by the destruction of the temple in 586 B.C. At this time "the whole race of his chosen root shall be dispersed"

(Enoch 93:8). "And after that in the seventh week shall an apostate generation arise. . . . At its close shall be elected the elect righteous of the eternal plant of righteousness" Enoch 93:9 f.). "And after that there shall be another, the eighth week, that of righteousness, and a sword shall be given to it. . . . And after that, in the ninth week, the righteous judgment shall be revealed to the whole world . . . the world shall be written down for destruction. . . . And after this, in the tenth week in the seventh part, there shall be the great eternal judgment, in which he will execute vengeance amongst the angels. And the first heaven shall depart and pass away, and a new heaven will appear" (Enoch 91:12–17). The author, who makes the seventh week begin with the exile and apparently believed that those who were left at the end of this week were to be counted among the elect righteous, does not say a word about any disappointment of his messianic expectation. Immediately after the election of "the elect righteous of the eternal plant of righteousness" there follows the time of salvation with its expected eschatological war of vengeance (cf. chap. IX.2,a). In this apocalyptic conception no place is left for an era of messianic travail. The apocalypse of the Seventy Shepherds, which may possibly be dated somewhat later, already contains some germs of this view. The sheep are attacked and hard pressed. Then there grows from the head of one of the sheep a great horn, which cannot be overthrown (90:9,12). But this horn must still withstand several attacks before the sheep are given a great sword of vengeance (90:19). Then follows a description of a final judgment and the new Jerusalem. The old house is folded up and its pillars are cast out. Then the Lord of the sheep "brought a new house greater and loftier than the first, and set it up in the place of the first" (90:28 f.). "And all that had been destroyed and dispersed . . . assembled in that house". And here too the sword which had been given to the sheep was laid down and sealed before the Lord (90:33 f.).

But the longer the expected end of the world was delayed the more did the conception of a "last age of wickedness" grow. Just before Satan is obliged to surrender he musters all his strength in order to bring the earth into his possession. And this he would succeed in doing, if the Qumrân community, the chosen remnant (cf. chap. IX,1,a), did not resist him. In this time of final struggle, however, Belial has more power over men than ever before. Then not only the conventional sins will increase but men will also make themselves guilty in a way that would have been inconceivable before. This is made especially clear in Enoch 100:1 f.: (In those days in one place the fathers together with their sons shall be smitten and brothers one with another shall fall in death till the streams flow with their blood. For a man shall not withhold his hand from slaying his sons and his sons' sons, and the sinner shall not withhold his hand from his honoured brother: from dawn till sunset they shall slay one another". And in 99:4 f. we read "In those days the nations shall be stirred up . . . the destitute shall go forth and carry off their children, and they shall abandon them, so that their children shall perish through them". In dependence upon the imagery of the Old Testament prophets, the pseudepigrapha familiar to the Qumrân circle also declare that the state of outward nature will also deteriorate on account of the sin of men. In Enoch 80:2 we read: "In the days of the sinners the years shall be shortened . . . all things on the earth shall alter, and shall not appear in their time: and the rain shall be kept back and the heaven shall withhold it".

Similarly in Jubilees 23:18: "The earth shall be destroyed on account of all their works, and there shall be no seed of the vine, and no oil; for their works are altogether faithless". In the Manual of Discipline 1:18 this time is called simply the "dominion of Belial" and in the Habakkuk Commentary 5:7 f. and the Damascus Document 6:10.14 it is called the "final era of wickedness". In the later rabbinical texts this closing period before the "days of the Messiah" is called the "travail of the messianic age". It was this view that preserved the community from being disillusioned by the disappointment of their expectation of the imminent coming of the Messiah and giving up hope of its fulfilment. The worse things became, the closer was the end. Thus no outward disaster could disabuse the members of the community of their trust in the imminence of the messianic future. A clear testimony of this confident faith of the community is found in the Habakkuk Commentary 7:7 f., 10–14: "This means that the very last period lasts a long time and extends longer than the prophets said; for the mysteries of God are marvellous. . . . This means the men of truth, who fulfil the law, whose hands do not grow slack in the service of the truth, when the final end is protracted beyond them; for all the last days of God will come according to their fixed order, even as he has [pre-]determined in the mysteries of his wisdom". Similarly, we read in the War Scroll 1:11 f.: "This is the time of strong tribulation for the people which God redeems, and in all its tribulations there has never been anything like it from the beginning to the consummation of the eternal redemption".

The last era of wickedness thus became an integral part of the eschatological conception of the Qumrân community; it became a part of the last days. In the time of religious persecution under Antiochus IV, the *Hasidim rishonim* had already expected the messianic event to occur in the immediate future, and now with the appearance of the Teacher of Righteousness (cf. chap. X) the messianic hopes were again inflamed and again disappointed, as is made fairly clear in Col. 7 of the Habakkuk Commentary. Thus, according to Hab. Comm. 2:7, the message of the Teacher affects "the last generation", while, according to the Damascus Document 1:11 f., he "made known to the last generations what God will do in the last generation to the congregation of the apostates". In accordance with this eschatological view, in the Qumrân texts the word *kes*, "end", is used for "time", for the real time is actually the time of the end. But in order to be able to distinguish the whole complex of the time of the final era, from the actual time of the end, the Habakkuk Commentary also speaks of the "end of the final era". In 7:1 f. we read: "And God told Habakkuk to write the things that were to come upon the last generation, but the end of the final era he did not [yet] make known to him." From these few passages cited here one can gain a good insight into the community's doctrine of the final era as it developed because of the delay of the end. The prophet Habakkuk, like the other prophets of the Old Testament too, can only make general statements about the end. This longer period of time the author of the commentary here calls "the last generation". the "end of the final era", which comes at the end of the "last generation", was made known by God to the Teacher of Righteousness (Hab. Comm. 7:4 f.). And yet, according to Hab. Com. 2:7, his message also affects the last generation, which here is apparently identical with the end of the final era; and in the Damascus Document 1:11 f. his message is definitely presented as being for the last generations; the end has therefore been delayed again. From this also it is clear how extraordinarily strong was the expectation of the Messiah in many Jewish circles in the time of Jesus.

The Qumrân Essenes' doctrine of the final age therefore possessed no strictly unified eschatological terminology, and, as it appears, the views of the community in these matters were also quite confused. It is certain, however that a yearning for redemption, a desire for a new world (cf. chap. IX,2,f), and a firm faith in the imminent restoration of the world in the new aeon were responsible for it. Nothing could dissuade the community from the firm conviction of faith that at the appointed time of his visitation God would exterminate evil for ever (Manual of Discipline 4:18 f.). But the end of wickedness will take an extremely drastic form. The community itself will march out to the final decisive war (cf. chap. IX,2,a), and the angels of God will come down to them from heaven (cf. chap. VIII,3,f). According to the picture drawn in the Hymn Scroll, earthquakes will then shake the earth and thunderstorms and seething floods of fire will pour down upon them: "The foundations of the wall will burst like a ship upon the high sea and the clouds will roar with thunder. The dwellers on earth and the voyagers on the sea will be terrified by the multitude of the waters" (3:13 f.). "When the lot points to judgment and the lot of anger falls upon the forsaken, and the outpouring of wrath upon the dissemblers, and it is the last period of anger for everything evil, then the pains of death are everywhere with no deliverance, and the torrents of Belial overflow all the banks [like] fire which devours all in its path, to destroy every green and dry tree in its channels, and it spreads out with flashing tongues, until nothing is left. It will eat at the foundations of the earth and the vaults of the bedrock, the pillars of the mountains will burn and the roots of the rock will become torrents of pitch. It will devour down to the great abyss and the torrents of Belial will burst into the underworld. The deepest depths of the sea will roar with the loud quaking of the mire, the earth will cry aloud at the outrage which is done to it. Then its pillars will burst and all who are upon it will go mad. They tremble at the great disaster, for God thunders in the fulness of his power and the heavenly throne of his holiness quakes in the truth of his majesty" (3:27–34). It is probably in this context that we should interpret the comment of Hippolytus in which he says that, according to the Essenes, a world conflagration will take place in the last days (*Adv. Haer.* 10,27).

d) The Length of the Last Age

In the context of the Qumrân Essenes' speculations upon the last age, the question of how long the end would last was also broached. In conformity with the forty years of wandering in the wilderness (Exod. 16:35), the same length of time was estimated for the duration of the last age. In the Commentary on Psalm 37 from Cave IV we read, in connection with verse 10: "Yet a little while, and the wicked will be no more; I(!) look at his place and the wicked one is no longer there: this refers to all wickedness, for when forty years have passed, there will be no wicked man on the earth." Correspondingly, according to the War Scroll 2:6–14, the final war in all its phases is to last for forty years (cf. chap. IX,2,a). Also in the Damascus Document 20:14 f. it is calculated that the time "from the day when the unique teacher [i.e., the Teacher of Righteousness, cf. chap. X] was gathered in until all the men of war who returned with the Man of the Lie are consumed will be about forty years." According to the Damascus Document 1:10 f., the Teacher of Righteousness came after the passage of half of the end period, that is, after twenty years. From these calculations too it can be seen that the community was forced to postpone the expected end. First the Teacher of Righteousness was to come in the first half of the end period, then they reckoned upon the forty years from the time when he was "gathered in", and finally the forty years were applied generally to the final war.

The number forty may possess a similar symbolism in the New Testament when it speaks of Jesus spending forty days fasting in the wilderness before he was tempted by the devil (Luke 4:2) and appearing to his disciples for forty days after his resurrection and before his ascension (Acts 1:3). Moses (Exod. 34:28) and Elijah (I Kings 19:8) are also said to have fasted for forty days.

e) Reward and Punishment at the Final Judgment and the Resurrection of the Dead

Although the Qumrân community was convinced, as the Hymn Scroll especially shows, that it was the elect remnant of the people of Israel (cf. chap. IX,1,a), it fervently awaited the last days with its judgment upon the evil and the reward of the good. Its members already knew that they were elected to salvation, but they were waiting for the eschatological realization of that salvation. This expectation is clearly stated in the Manual of Discipline 4:7,8,12–14: "[The destiny of the good is] abundance of peace in length of days, fruition of seed with all the blessings of eternity, everlasting joy in the life of eternity and the crown of [divine] glory with its splendour in everlasting light. . . . [The destiny of the evil] leads to abundance of afflictions by all the destroying angels, to eternal perdition in the overflowing, avenging wrath of God, to everlasting maltreatment and to perpetual reproach, with the disgrace of annihilation in the fire of hell. And the whole end of their generations [will be] in sorrowful mourning and [there will be] bitter hardship when the destruction of darkness [strikes them], until they are utterly exterminated to the last remnant." In the Damascus Document 2:5 f. too, divine punishment "in flames of fire", which will be carried out by the destroying angels, is proclaimed to the rebellious and the despisers of the law. The concept of hell also plays a large role in the pseudepigrapha belonging to the Qumrân sphere. We come near to getting the impression that the Romanic and Gothic artists found the inspiration for their representations of the last judgment in these and similar pictures. Thus we read in Enoch 10:13: "In those days they shall be led off to the abyss of fire, and to the torment and the prison in which they shall be confined for ever." 90:26: "And I saw at that time how a like abyss was opened in the midst of the earth, full of fire . . . and they were all judged and found guilty and cast into the fiery abyss." 100:9: "Woe to you sinners, for ye shall burn in flaming fire." 103:8: "Into darkness and chains and a burning flame shall your spirits enter when the great judgment takes place. Woe to you, for ye shall have no peace." Similarly, we read in Enoch 27:1–3: "Then said I: 'For what object is this blessed land, which is entirely filled with trees, and this accursed valley between!' Then Urial, one of the holy angels who was with me, answered and said, 'This accursed valley is for those who are accursed for ever . . . here shall be their place of judgment. In the last days there shall be upon them the spectacle of a righteous judgment in the presence of the righteous for ever'."

The description of the eschatological glory in the Book of Enoch, like the depiction of hell, exhibits parallels to the Manual of Discipline. Such a detailed description is found in Enoch 10:16–22: "Let every evil work come to an end; and let the plant of righteousness and truth appear . . . the works of righteousness and truth shall be planted in truth and joy for evermore. And then shall all the righteous escape, and shall live till they beget thousands of children, and all the days of their youth and their old age shall they complete in peace. And then shall the whole earth be tilled in righteousness. . . . And all desirable trees shall be planted on it, and they shall plant vines on it; and the vine which they plant thereon shall yield wine in abundance. . . . And the earth shall be cleansed from all defilement, and from all sin, and from all punishment, and from all torment . . . from generation to generation and for ever."

The Qumrân Essenes envisaged both reward and punishment in extremely anthropomorphic images. They therefore believed in a continuance of physical existence after death or a new bodily existence at the last judgment. This conception presupposes at least a rudimentary belief in a resurrection of the dead. It is true that Josephus Flavius in *Ant.* 18,1,5 speaks only of an Essenic belief in the immortality of the soul, but this way of putting it may be no more than a concession to his Greek readers. This tendency is even more apparent in *Bellum* 2,8,11, where he reconciles the Essene teachings concerning the life beyond to the Greek conception of the islands of the blessed: "The good are assigned to a life beyond the ocean, in a place that is neither oppressed with rain or snow or with heat.

... The evil, however, they assign to a dark cave of eternal torments." Josephus' Hellenizing manner of presentation is therefore to be fundamentally mistrusted, for the Essenes were not a Hellenistic, syncretistic group, but rather a Jewish apocalyptic movement. The Old Testament prophets had already described the last days in extremely worldly images. For the prophets the end is a cleansed and purified "this world" and not a colourless beyond. This "this worldly"-oriented eschatological expectation is even more clearly expressed in the apocalypses, since the apocalyptists awaited the dawn of the coming world with a fervent desire which was increased by the defectiveness of the present world. So by an inner logic it follows that their conception of life after death and life in a new aeon could not be spiritualized but had to become even more materialistic. Moreover, it is a well known fact that the rudimentary hope expressed in those passages of the Old Testament which speak of a resurrection of the dead has become, in apocalypticism, the resurrection hope itself. To be sure, this hope naturally developed slowly and was not yet formulated in dogmatic terms. As elsewhere in the ancient east, it was simply impossible for them to conceive of a life without a body, and therefore the life beyond must also be a physical life. Not until, under Greek influence, the conception of a continuing existence of the soul alone had found adherents in Palestinian Judaism did the rabbis see the necessity in the first and second centuries after Christ of formulating the resurrection of the dead as an article of faith (Sanhedrin X,1,2, *helek*). But even at that time the conceptions were by no means uniform, since the beyond for the righteous was conceived of either in completely anthropomorphic terms, or in more spiritualized terms, and also with regard to the wicked the punishment of hell was assumed to be either perpetual or transitory; and furthermore, the opinion prevailed that certain groups of sinners would not participate at all in the resurrection for judgment.

Thus even in Pharisaic Judaism up to the Talmudic period the concept of the resurrection continued to remain fairly diverse, though the expectation of resurrection was generally accepted and disseminated. Consequently, it is not to be expected that the Qumrân texts and the pseudepigrapha extant in the Qumrân sphere will make dogmatically binding statements about the resurrection of the dead. The hope of resurrection is expressed as early as Daniel 12:2, in a text, therefore, which is undoubtedly to be dated prior to the Qumrân sect. It was therefore already known to the *Hasidim rishonim*, the group from which the Qumrân community emerged (cf. chap. VII). Thus in II Macc. 7:9–14 three of the seven martyred brothers are made to say: "Thou, miscreant, dost release us out of this present life, but the King of the world shall raise up us, who have died for his laws, unto an eternal renewal of life. . . . From him I hope to receive these [hands] back again. . . . It is good to die at the hands of men and look for the hopes which are given by God, that we shall be raised up again by him; for as for thee, thou shalt have no resurrection unto life." We mention only a few examples from the pseudepigrapha extant in the Qumrân sphere. In the Testament of Judah 25,4 we read: "They who have died in grief shall arise in joy;" and in the Testament of Zebulun 10:1–3: "And now, my children, grieve not that I am dying . . . for I shall rise again in the midst of you. . . . But upon the ungodly shall the Lord bring eternal fire, and destroy them throughout all generations." Enoch 92:3: "The righteous man will arise from the sleep of death." Correspondingly, we read in the Hymn Scroll 11:12 that God will "raise the worms of the dead from the dust." It is clearly evident from these texts that at least the righteous shall rise again. But the fate of the wicked shall be "reproach and extinction in the fires of hell." But with regard to the time when these punishments of hell are to begin and how long they are to last, these texts give us no clear answer, and we get the impression that in these matters the opinions of the community also were very divergent.

Though the resurrection of the righteous was most often conceived as a bodily resurrection, the opposite view is also documented in the Book of Jubilees 23:30 f.: "And at that time the Lord will heal his servants, and they will rise up and see a great peace, and drive out their adversaries. . . . And their bones will rest in the earth and their spirits will have much joy." But that the view here represented of a bodiless state in the new world was not meant literally is clear from the two preceding verses: "And there will be no old man nor one who is not satisfied with his days, for all will be [as] children and youths. And all their days they will complete and live in peace and in joy, and there will be no Satan nor any evil destroyer."

To sum up, therefore, we can be sure that the anthropomorphic views of the beyond and the last days led the Qumrân Essenes to believe in the continuance of bodily existence even though they reckoned on the passing of the body itself. From these beginnings, in the course of time there developed the resurrection hope, formulated as an article of faith.

f) The New Creation

In the Manual of Discipline 4:25 we read that God permits the two forces of light and darkness to work in equal measure on earth "until the determined end and until the new creation" (cf. chap. VIII,3,f.) Hence the state after the destruction of evil is described as the new creation. This view is also familiar to the Book of Enoch. According to Enoch 91:16, the first heaven will disappear and a new heaven will appear. And 90:29 speaks of a new Jerusalem and a new temple. Moreover, in the year 1949 the excavators found in Cave I a number of very small fragments which, to all appearances, describe the new Jerusalem. It follows from these references that the Qumrân community cherished the hope of a re-ordering of the cosmos which would remove all the imperfections of the present aeon (cf. chap. IX,2,c) for ever. This new order was the goal of their apocalyptic speculations. This idea was then further developed in the later apocalypses which are no longer within the broader scope of the Essene texts.

X

THE TEACHER OF RIGHTEOUSNESS
AND THE TWO MESSIAHS

THE messianic expectations of the Qumrân community are summed up in one sentence in the Manual of Discipline 9:10 f.: "They shall be judged according to the earlier statutes of the law, by which the men of the community began to discipline themselves, until the coming of the Prophet and the Messiahs from Aaron and Israel." This clearly shows that the Qumrân Essenes expected three messianic functionaries: two messiahs and a prophet. The expectation of a messianic *prophet* was not only generally known in the New Testament but is also alluded to in the Old Testament. Deut. 18:15,18 contains the announcement of a new prophet who will be like Moses. In Mal. 4:5 the return of the prophet Elijah is announced. His task will be the reconciliation of men. He must "turn the hearts of fathers to their children and the hearts of children to their fathers" (4:6). His function is therefore to create the human disposition for the messianic age by moving the sinners to repentance. In I Maccabees there are two valuable pieces of evidence for the expectation of a messianic prophet in the second century before Christ. These two references show that the last prophet would also have to answer questions on religious law, which probably means that in him was expected the ultimately competent interpreter of the Mosaic law. According to I Macc. 4:46, he is to decide

113

about the stones of the altar of burnt offering defiled by the Syrians: "The stones, however, they laid up in the Mountain of the Temple in a convenient place, until there should come a prophet who could give an answer concerning them." And in September, 141 B.C., when the highest spiritual and secular power was awarded to the Hasmonean Simon and his descendants by the people, this resolution was framed to remain in force until it should be revoked by the messianic prophet: "And now the Jews and the priests gave their consent that Simon should be their leader and high priest for ever, until there should arise a trustworthy prophet" (I Macc. 14:41).

For the Qumrân Essenes the *Teacher of Righteousness* was this expected last prophet. According to the Habakkuk Commentary 7:4 f., "God made known to him all the mysteries of the words of his servants the prophets." The context indicates that these mysteries were primarily of an eschatological character. The Teacher was for his community the proclaimer of the approaching end of the world (cf. chap. IX,2,c). Correspondingly, the Damascus Document 1:11 f. says of him that "he made known to the later generations what God will do in the last generation to the congregation of the apostates." But things did not turn out the way the Teacher of Righteousness had predicted. The end delayed despite his message. Some were doubtless disillusioned as to his prophetic mission. In the Habakkuk Commentary 5:9–11 reproaches are directed at an apostate group called the house of Absolom, which —apparently contrary to the expectation of the community —had not helped the Teacher against the Man of the Lie. On the other hand, in 8:1 f., those who have been faithful to the law and who have believed in his message and dignity, are again assured "that God will rescue them from

the place of judgment." From 11:4–8 we gather that the
Teacher had fled and was pursued into his "house of
exile" by the Wicked Priest who desired to "swallow him
up in the fury of his anger". This whole event took place
on a day which for the community was the day of atonement, the greatest day of festival and rest, but which was
an ordinary weekday for the Wicked Priest, since the
Qumrân Essenes and the rest of Judaism had two different
calendars (cf. chap. VIII,2,d). Some interpreters believe
that the Teacher was killed by the Wicked Priest on this
or some other occasion. This interpretation is possible, but
on the basis of the texts hitherto available by no means
conclusive. Two important passages in the Damascus
Document, 8:21 b and 20:14, say only that he was
"gathered in". His faithful followers, however, were not
led astray by this and believed that he would return again
at the end of the end. Thus in the Damascus Document
6:10 f., we read: "But without which they will understand
nothing, until the Teacher of Righteousness arises [again]
in the last days."

From a comparison of the Habakkuk Commentary
2:5–9 with 7:4 f. and from the Commentary on Psalm 37
from Cave IV it appears that the Teacher of Righteousness, like John the Baptist later, was descended from a
priestly family. The Testament of Levi 2:10 also speaks of
a priestly prophet of the last age: "Thou shalt stand near
the Lord, and shalt be his minister, and shalt declare his
mysteries to men, and shalt proclaim concerning him that
shall redeem Israel." The Testament of Benjamin 9:2 says
that "the Most High shall send forth his salvation under
the supervision of the one prophet." Because the Teacher
came from a priestly family some scholars have identified
him with the Priest-Messiah. According to this view the

Teacher is therefore supposed to be both the messianic prophet and the Messiah from Aaron. Against this interpretation, however, is the formula from the Manual of Discipline cited at the beginning of this chapter, which mentions one prophet and the Messiahs from Aaron and Israel. Hence the prophet cannot very well be identified with the two Messiahs. Furthermore, the time indication mentioned in the Damascus Document 8:21 b, f., "from the day when the teacher of the community [i.e. the Teacher of Righteousness] was gathered in until the coming of the Messiah[s] from Aaron and Israel", would be hardly intelligible if the Teacher and the Priest-Messiah from Aaron were the same person. The only way out of this difficulty would be the assumption that originally the Teacher was indeed the messianic prophet, but that after his return he would be the messianic high priest. The texts now available, however, provide no grounds for such an interpretation.

The Old Testament basis for the *doctrine of the two Messiahs* is furnished by the saying of Baalam in Numbers 24:17 b: "A star shall come forth out of Jacob, and a sceptre shall rise out of Israel." The Qumrân Essenes identified the star with the Priest-Messiah and the sceptre with the Davidic Lay-Messiah. This saying of Balaam is cited in a number of passages in the Qumrân texts and the Testaments of the Twelve Patriarchs as a basis for the community's eschatological certainty of salvation and it is very probable that in every instance it is intended as a reference to the two Messiahs. There are also several instances in which the symbols of the star and sceptre are used as attributes of the Priest-Messiah and the Lay-Messiah.

In all ritual and religious concerns the Priest-Messiah is

ranked above the Lay-Messiah, just as the priests always ranked above the laity in cultic matters. The Book of Rules 2:11–21 speaks of a ritual meal (cf. chap. VIII,3,a), which is to take place in the messianic age: "And this is the seating order of the men of the 'Name', those called at the 'appointed time', for the council of the community, in case God permits the Messiah [i.e., the Lay-Messiah] to be with them: First comes the Priest, the head of the entire community of Israel [i.e., the Priest-Messiah], and all the fathers of the sons of Aaron, the priests, those called at the 'appointed time', the men of the 'Name', and they take their places before him, each according to his rank. Then the Messiah from Israel [i.e., the Lay-Messiah] takes his place and before him the chiefs of the thousands of Israel take their place, each according to his rank, corresponding to his position in their camps and marches. And all the heads of the fathers of the community, together with the wise men of the congregation of holiness take their places before them, each according to his rank. And when they gather at the table of the community, or [assemble themselves] to drink the wine, the table of the community is to be spread. At the pouring of the wine for drinking no one is to reach out his hand for the bread and the wine before the Priest [i.e., the Priest-Messiah], for it is he who first blesses the bread and the wine and first reaches out his hand to the bread. Then the Messiah from Israel reaches out his hands for the bread, and after that all the members of the community say the blessing, each according to his rank." The same idea is found in the Testaments of the Twelve Patriarchs. There the name of Levi, the progenitor of the priestly families, represents the Highpriestly Messiah, while the name of Judah refers to the Davidic Lay-Messiah. Thus we read in the Testa-

ment of Simeon 7:1 f.: "And now, my children, obey Levi
and Judah, and be not lifted up against these two tribes,
for from them shall arise unto you the salvation of God.
For the Lord shall raise up from Levi as it were a High-
priest, and from Judah as it were a king." And even
more clearly in the Testament of Judah 21:1–3: "And
now, my children, I command you, love Levi . . . for to
me the Lord gave the kingdom, and to him the priesthood,
and he set the kingdom beneath the priesthood. To me he
gave the things upon the earth; to him the things in the
heavens." The Testament of Reuben 6:8 also speaks expressly of a Highpriestly Messiah: "Therefore I command
you to hearken to Levi, because he shall know the law of
the Lord, and shall give ordinances for judgment and shall
sacrifice for all Israel until the consummation of the High-
priestly Messiah."

The *Lay-Messiah* was therefore to come from the tribe
of Judah, i.e., the lineage of David; he was to be the awaited
son of David. In the Qumrân texts he is not only compared
with the sceptre, which, according to Gen. 49:10, "shall
not depart from Judah", but is also described with other
Davidic, messianic attributes from the Old Testament. In
the commentary on the Patriarchal Blessings from Cave IV
he is called "the Messiah of righteousness, scion [cf. Jer.
23:5; 33:15; Zech. 3:8; 6:12] of David", and in the fragmentary songs of praise, which apparently belong to the
Book of Rules, he is called, according to Ezekiel
34:24; 37:25, "prince of the community." The Damascus
Document 7:20 f. says of him: "The sceptre is the prince
of the whole congregation, and when he arises he shall
break down all the sons of Seth." It is the task of this prince
of the congregation, who is introduced in the above-
mentioned fragmentary songs of praise with Davidic,

messianic attributes taken from Isa. 11:2–5 and Mic. 4:13, to "establish the kingdom of his people," i.e., to establish the kingdom of God on earth. The Davidic Messiah is therefore the militant Messiah. And this is the reason why, according to the Book of Rules 2:14 f., the Messiah of Israel enters the assembly hall at the head of the chiefs of the thousands of Israel, i.e., the generals. He is the commander-in-chief of the community, since the priests, who were otherwise always at the head of the community, were not allowed to take part in the battles, lest they be defiled by the blood of the slain. Thus we read in the War Scroll 9:7–9: "When the 'slain' fall, then the priests shall trumpet from a distance and not go up to the slain, in order not to defile themselves with the blood of their uncleanness; for they are holy and they must not profane the anointing oil of their priesthood with the blood of the vain [i.e. not relevant to the history of salvation] nations." The craft of war is therefore the affair of the laity and thus in military matters the Lay-Messiah, the 'prince of the whole congregation," takes precedence, whereas in ritual matters the Priest-Messiah is supreme. Hence according to the War Scroll 5:1, on the shield of the prince the name of Israel is written first and then those of Levi and Aaron. Likewise, according to 3:13, on the "great standard at the head of the whole people" the name of Israel is written first and then the name of Aaron.

In conjunction with the prophecy of Nathan to David in II Sam. 7:11–14, the Qumrân Essenes may also have been of the opinion that the messianic scion of David was identified with the pre-existent, hidden Son of God. Thus we read in the Messianic Florilegium from Cave IV: "The Lord made known to you that he will build a house for you: I will raise up thy seed after you and establish the throne of his kingdom for ever. I will be his father and he shall be my son. This is the scion of David, who arises with the teacher of the Torah [i.e., the Priest-Messiah], who will spring up in Zion in the last days, as it is written: I will raise up the booth of David that is fallen [Amos 9:11]. This is the falling booth of David and to this end he will arise in order to redeem Israel." Jesus' controversy with the Pharisaic scribes concerning the messianic interpretation of Psalm 110:1 (Matt. 22:41–5; Mark 12:35–7; Luke 20:41–4) may probably be understood in this context. Also in IV Ezra, which appeared shortly after the destruction of Jerusalem in A.D. 70 and therefore cannot belong to the immediate sphere of the Qumrân Essenes, it is implied that the "Son of God" and the "Son of David" of the last age are one and the same. In IV Ezra 12:31 f. we read: "And as for the lion . . . this is the Messiah whom the Most High hath kept unto the last days, who shall spring from the seed of David," and in IV Ezra 7:28: "For my [i.e., God's] Son the Messiah, the anointed, shall be revealed together with those who are with him, and shall rejoice the survivors for four hundred years."

One of the most difficult messianic passages is to be found in the Hymn Scroll 3:9 f., where we read: "And the pregnancy with the 'man of affliction' is in its throes, for amid the throes of death will she [i.e., the community, which is being compared to a pregnant woman in the throes of childbirth] give birth to a man-child and amid the throes of the underworld with the 'Wonderful Counsellor with his might' [Isa. 9:5] burst forth from the crucible of pregnancy and the 'Man' goes forth unscathed from the throes of the womb." Here it is not impossible, in view of the Servant of God prophecies (Isa. 49:1,5; 52: 13–53:12), to think of a suffering Messiah. On the other hand, however, the term "man of affliction" may refer only to the travails at his birth. A very obscure passage in the Testament of Reuben 6:10–12 may, however, be interpreted in the sense of the suffering of the Davidic Messiah. There it is said of Judah, and hence of the Messiah of the house of David; "Bow down before his seed, for on your behalf it will die in wars visible and invisible." But since it is not certain whether this passage is original or a later Christian addition, it cannot be regarded as conclusive. Hence we shall have to wait for further publications of the texts before we can give a final answer to the question whether the Davidic Messiah—like the later Messiah Son of Joseph of the rabbis—was not only to struggle, but also fall, and perhaps even suffer.

XI

THE RISE OF CHRISTIANITY
AND THE QUMRÂN TEXTS

In this chapter we can mention only the most important identities, similarities, and differences between the teachings of the Qumrân community and those of the New Testament. An exhaustive examination of this problem would have to be the subject of a separate and detailed treatise. Nevertheless, even this brief section will indicate the extraordinarily great significance of the Qumrân finds for the religious and historical understanding of the New Testament. One can say without exaggeration that in this respect the Qumrân texts are the most important discoveries yet made. But when we here point out similarities and identities, this does not mean that we are asserting that in all cases a direct dependence of the New Testament conceptions upon the corresponding Qumrân Essene views either must or can be assumed. The Qumrân Essenes represented only a part of the general apocalyptic movement in Judaism and they are not to be identified in every respect with this movement. Among their specific peculiarities belongs the priestly element which is strongly emphasized in the Qumrân texts (cf. chap. VII including, among others, the great interest in the questions concerning the cultus, the problems of the calendar, and the ritual lustrations, cf. chap. VIII, 3,b–d). Besides this there were circles in which the expectation of the Son of Man was disseminated. This can be related only indirectly to the political expectation of a Davidic Messiah which had a different religious and historical origin, different also from that of the Zealots, who were not waiting for the last days for a war of God, but wanted to begin it at once. One must therefore be on one's guard against overstating the value of the Qumrân texts simply because of the joy of discovery and believing that they can give us a complete picture of the messianic movement at the time of Jesus. Nevertheless, like the New Testament, they do belong within the framework of this movement. From the Qumrân texts we therefore in many respects come to know the spiritual atmosphere in which lived John the Baptist, the followers of Jesus, and the first members of the primitive church. Only now, therefore, are many passages of the Gospels put in the right religious, historical light.

Again and again we encounter the objection that the New Testament says nothing of the Essenes and that it is therefore a very strange thing to be told that the New Testament and the Essenes stem from the same roots. I regard this objection to be neither convincing nor justified. We do not even know how the Essenes received this name or whether they themselves ever used it at all. The word "Essaioi" may be the Greek transcription of the Aramaic word *chasaia*, meaning "the pious". The term "Essene" would then correspond to the root-form of the same word which in Aramaic is *chasen*. Among the numerous names which the Qumrân people applied to themselves, at least in the hitherto known texts, the term *chasaia* or *chasen* does not occur a single time; and yet the close relationship between the Qumrân community and other Essenic groups appears to be beyond all doubt (cf. chap. VIII). This fact

proves that the term "Essene" was by no means characteristic of those groups which are so named by the
classical writers.

Thus it is necessary for us to examine more closely the
sources which describe the background of Judaism in the
time of Jesus. There are three groups of such sources:
(1) the Hellenistic authors and the church writers. These
writers distinguish between three "Jewish parties", Pharisees, Sadducees, and Essenes. (2) The Talmudic rabbinical
literature. Here again, if we disregard double names for
certain groups, we encounter three factions: Pharisees,
Sadducees, and Hasidim rishonim (cf. chaps. VI,2; and
VII). (3) The New Testament also mentions Pharisees and
Sadducees. A third and less homogenous group consists
of those who were looking for the coming "kingdom of
God", in other words, those who lived in an acute
messianic expectation. To these belonged the adherents of
John the Baptist as well as the apostles and disciples of
Jesus. Since the Pharisees and Sadducees are the same in
all three groups of sources, it seems natural to regard the
three different appellations of the third group as three
different aspects of one and the same group. But this group
as such was by no means tightly organized; it was perhaps
only a loose fellowship of people, a group of groups which
were held together by nothing more than a common acute
messianic expectation. Hence the New Testament appella-
tion for this mass of people who were stirred by messianic
expectation may well be the most apposite one. The
Sadducees and the Pharisees, for different reasons in each
case, and unlike the followers of the Baptist, Jesus, and
the Zealots, did not belong to these groups. When a
Pharisee "looked for the kingdom of God", this is mentioned in the New Testament as an exception to the rule

(e.g., Mark 15:43, cf. Luke 23:50; Matt. 27:57; John 19:38; John 3:1–5).

The Talmudic literature presents the same picture. No acute messianic statements by the scholars of the first Tannaitic generation, who were contemporaries of Jesus, have been preserved. Messianic expectation at the time of Jesus was limited to the circle of popular prophets and to the apocalpytists who were emphatically rejected by Pharisaism (cf. chap. VII). The pseudepigrapha were deliberately omitted from the canon by the Pharisees (cf. chap. II). Not until after the destruction of Jerusalem in A.D. 70, in fact really not until the second century after Christ do we find acute messianic teachings in the circles of Pharisaic rabbis; and yet at the same time there were also counter-movements which made the disappointment over the collapse of the rebellion of Bar Kokhba (A.D. 132–135) bearable.

These brief references make it clear that the messianic groups may, to the extent that they stood in common opposition to Pharisaism and Sadduceeism, be regarded as a unity precisely because of their common messianic expectation and despite their inner differences. For the New Testament, however, these groups are interesting solely because of their expectation of the Messiah. Neither their legalistic piety, documented in the Qumrân texts and reported in relation to the Hasidim rishonim in the Talmud, nor the monastic attitude of the Essenes, which was considered especially important by Philo, Josephus, and Pliny, was of any vital interest to the New Testament authors. Accordingly, when the New Testament speaks of those who looked for the "kingdom of God", the Essenes are probably included among them.

I. THE QUMRÂN TEXTS AND JOHN THE BAPTIST

John the Baptist was undoubtedly in close contact with the teachings of the Qumrân Essenes. Like them, he proclaimed the immediately imminent last days, the "kingdom of God" (cf. chap. X,2,c; Matt. 3:1–3; Mark 1:2–4; Luke 3:1–4; John 1:19,23). His sojourn in the wilderness and that of the Qumrân Essenes were both inspired by the summons of Isa. 40:3: "A voice cries: 'In the wilderness prepare the way of the Lord, make straight in the desert a highway for our God'." (cf. chap. VI,2.) The place where John baptized in the Jordan, just before it flows into the Dead Sea, was not far from the monastery of Qumrân, which was then in its second flowering (cf. chap. V). In these circumstances it is inconceivable that there was no contact between the two. Nevertheless, one cannot call John the Baptist an Essene or a dissident Essene without qualification for his message and his practice went far beyond the bounds of the Essenes.

John was born of a priestly family. Both his father Zacharias and his mother Elizabeth were of priestly descent (Luke 1:5). The core of the Qumrân community also consisted of priests (cf. chaps, VI,1a; VII), who, however, had dissociated themselves from the Jerusalem cultus, because in their eyes it was administered by unworthy priests and according to a false calendar (cf. chap. VIII, 3,c,d). On the other hand, however, it is expressly stated of Zacharias that he performed his cultic functions in the temple of Jerusalem (Luke 1:8 f.). With the one exception of the relationship with the Jerusalem temple, however, there is much that is reported in the first two chapters of the Gospel of Luke which fits in better with the spiritual background of the Qumrân priests than with the temple priesthood of Jerusalem. The Qumrân priests lived in acute expectation of the imminent coming of the Messiah; and Zacharias too is said to have been "filled with the Holy Spirit" and praised the God of Israel "for he has visited and redeemed his people" (Luke 1:67 f.).

According to the opinion of the Pharisees, however, after the death of Malachi, the last of the minor prophets, the Holy Spirit and the gift of prophecy disappeared from Israel (cf. chap. II), and the Sadduceean priests were even further removed from the apocalyptic attitude than the Pharisees. On the other hand, the writer of the nativity and childhood story in the first two chapters of the Gospel of Luke is quite unaware of the view that there was no more prophecy in Israel. Here there is prophesying on every hand, and all these prophecies are related to the immediately imminent messianic event. Both the aged Simeon, who looked "for the consolation of Israel" and the ascetic prophetess Anna proclaimed that the child Jesus was the expected redeemer (Luke 2:25–38). But all this took place in the temple of Jerusalem, which was shunned by the Qumrân people. Both the Benedictus of Zacharias (Luke 1:68–75) and the Magnificat of Mary (Luke 1:46–55) are strongly reminiscent both in style and content of the Qumrân hymns. These agreements and differences indicate that Zacharias and his circle were probably familiar with the views of the Qumrân Essenes, but that he himself lived in peace with the official temple priesthood. This circumstance in itself should make us cautious about identifying the Qumrân sect with the messianic movement as such.

John himself may well have been more radical than his father. No mention is made anywhere about his taking part in the temple cult. In the light of all that the Gospels say about John, such participation appears to be very improbable. He had approached the messianic ideal of the wilderness even more than had his parents. Even as a child he lived in the desert, where apparently he was brought up, and it was in the desert that the prophetic call came to him (Luke 1:80; 3:2). Hence it is conceivable that he may have lived with the Qumrân Essenes. Josephus reports that the Essenes adopted the children of others (*Bellum* 2,8,2). But if John spent his youth among the Essenes, it is surprising, to say the least, that Josephus should leave this fact wholly unmentioned in his detailed account of John the Baptist in *Ant.* 18,5,2. Moreover, it was not only the Essenes who lived in the desert. In the second chapter of his autobiography Josephus gives an account of a certain Banus, "who lived in the desert, wore clothing made of tree bark, ate wild herbs, and washed himself with cold water frequently during the day as well as at night for purification." In Josephus' account this Banus is clearly distinguished from the Essenes. The food and clothing of Banus remind us of the picture of John given in Matt. 3:4: "Now John wore a garment of camel's hair, and a leather girdle around his waist; and his food was locusts and wild honey." But here again the washings of Banus have more in common with the lustrations of the Essenes (cf. chap. VIII,3,b) than with John's baptism for the forgiveness of sins.

The messianic message of John, like the community theology of the Qumrân Essenes, was imbued with the idea of repentance. If the latter regarded themselves as the penitents of the Israel of the last days (cf. chap. IX, 1,a end), John too called men to repentance (Matt. 3:6; Mark 1:4; Luke 3:3) because the "kingdom of God" was already near. But, unlike the Qumrân people, John was not a founder of a sect. Whereas the Qumrân Essenes withdrew from the rest of Israel, which they regarded as a *massa damnata,* John addressed himself to the whole of Israel. The people of Jerusalem, Judaea, and the region of the Jordan went out to hear his preaching (Matt. 3:5; Mark 1:5). In contrast with the Qumrân Essenes, John did not gather about him all those whom he had baptized and establish a congregation of penitents, but discharged most of them after baptism. Only a few disciples may have remained with him. Nor did it require any long preparation before being admitted to baptism, as was required by the monastic Essenes of their novices (cf. chap. VIII,2,a). The baptism of John was apparently a single, non-recurring act of repentance and therefore different in nature from the ritual baths of the Essenes. Ultimately, it was also because of his particular kind of baptism that John was called "the Baptist". Nevertheless, the baptism of John could have been a further development of the ritual lustrations of the Qumrân Essenes, just as these were no more than a further development of the Old Testament Levitical purification customs.

John baptized with water, but promised the coming of one who would be mightier than he, who would baptize with the Holy Spirit and with fire (Matt. 3:11; Mark 1:8; Luke 3:16). It is possible to see in this an allusion to an expected judgment of fire at the end of time, which the Qumrân Essenes also contemplated (cf. chap. IX,2c, end). Like the Qumrân Essenes, John too was decidedly anti-Pharisaic and anti-Sadducaic (cf. chap. I,3,i—Hab. Com.; chap. VII). Thus, for example, he called his opponents a "brood of vipers", who would not escape the wrath to come if they did not repent (Matt. 3:7; Luke 3:7).

However, John's view, that God could raise up children to Abraham from stones (Matt. 3:7–9; Luke 3:7 f.), expressed in connection with his polemic against the Pharisees and Sadducees, is in radical contradiction to the Qumrân Essenes' doctrine of election (cf. chap. IX,1,a), in which the non-Jews are summed up in the term "vain heathen", i.e., heathen who have no relevance to the history of salvation (War Scroll 9:9; 11:9).

Corresponding to the Qumrân doctrine of the Messiah, in which, in association with Deut. 18:15,18 and Mal. 3:23, a messianic prophet was expected to come before the advent of the messianic period itself (cf. chap. X), John the Baptist may also have been considered to be such a prophet by the congregation of Jesus (Matt. 11:9–14; 17:12). According to John 1:21, he himself rejected this claim, and yet the historical value of this passage is doubtful. According to Matt. 3:11–17; Mark 1:7–11; Luke 3:16–22; John 1:26–34, John is said to have pointed to one who would come after him and the thong of whose sandals he was unworthy to untie. And when Jesus came to him at the Jordan, he said to him, according to Matt. 3:14: "I need to be baptized by you, and do you come to me?" Regardless of whether one considers these statements as historical or as the result of the Christological views current in the primitive church, they should be related to the teaching of the Qumrân Essenes that a priestly and a Davidic Messiah were to come and that the latter is subordinate to the former in cultic matters (cf. chap. X). So that when the Davidic Jesus comes to the priest John at the Jordan and subjects himself to his baptism for the forgiveness of sins, this must necessarily create the impression that he subordinated himself to the latter. The clear statement of John that he himself is less worthy than the

Jesus whom he baptized therefore appears, in the light of the Qumrân Essene Two-Messiahs doctrine, to be altogether intelligible and necessary for the Gospel tradition.

The general ascetic attitude of John the Baptist and his disciples and the justified assumption that he also remained unmarried bring him again into very close relationship with the monastic ideal of the Essenes. Are we then to seek for the spiritual origins of John among the Qumrân Essenes in general or among the Qumrân Essenes in particular, or do the available sources permit us only to classify him in the broader framework of the messianic movement within which he and his disciples were one group among many? The latter can no doubt be maintained with certainty, and yet, as the arguments stated above indicate, it appears to be practically certain that he was acquainted with the Qumrân Essene teachings and that he had come to grips with them. A direct, temporary membership in the Qumrân community itself is quite conceivable, but by no means absolutely certain.

2. THE JESUS OF THE GOSPEL TRADITION IN THE LIGHT OF THE QUMRÂN TEXTS

a) The General Eschatological Expectation

Like John, Jesus too proclaimed the advent of the kingdom of God. His circle too was imbued with the expectation of the imminent coming of the Messiah. In Luke 4:1 we read: "And Jesus, full of the Holy Spirit, returned from the Jordan, and was led by the Spirit for forty days in the wilderness" (cf. Matt. 4:1; Mark 1:12). In the wilderness he fasted for forty days and was tempted by the devil. The number forty is doubtless to be understood schematically (cf. chap. IX,2,d). The three temptations of the devil are all eschatological in intention. Jesus was supposed to reveal himself clearly as a messianic miracle-worker, so that there could be no doubt of his messiah-ship. *Faith* in the Messiah was to be transformed into *knowledge* of the Messiah. Jesus was to prove himself to be the Messiah of the messianic movement with its hope of an imminent coming.

Closely connected with this, the Gospel of Luke gives an account of Jesus' clash with the people of Nazareth in the synagogue of his home city (Luke 4:14-30. cf. Matt. 13: 54-8; Mark 6:1-5). There on the sabbath a scroll of the Scriptures was handed to him. In the lesson for the week was the passage Isaiah 61:1, in which eschatological liberty is proclaimed to the "poor". According to the War Scroll of Qumrân, the "poor" are said to be God's instruments of salvation in the last days; into their hands God will "deliver the enemies of all lands" (cf. chap. IX, 1,b). According to Matt. 11:5 and Luke 7:22, Jesus himself interpreted the verse, Isa. 61:1, messianically when he cited the passage to the disciples of John who were inquiring about his Messiahship on behalf of their imprisoned master. Therefore at the beginning they were disappointed when Jesus "closed the book, and gave it to the attendant, and sat down" (Luke 4:20). Graphically, the Gospel of Luke reads that then "the eyes of all in the synagogue were fixed on him". Addressing himself to this searching gaze, Jesus began to interpret the passage as acutely messianic: "To-day this scripture has been ful-filled in your hearing" (4:21). This declaration transported his countrymen into a state of messianic enthusiasm (4:22). But Jesus could not and would not satisfy these massive messianic hopes which reposed in him. And the people of Nazareth were filled with anger. The enthusiasm suddenly turned into hatred and they tried to throw Jesus down from the hill on which the city is built (4:29).

This episode in the synagogue of Nazareth demonstrates to us how widespread in Palestinian Judaism was the acute expectation of the last days to which the Qumrân texts bear witness. Despite many postponements, the messianic event was expected to occur in the very near future (cf. chap. IX,2,c). In this context too belong the so-called announcements of the Passion (Matt. 16:21; 17:22–33; 20:17–19; 26:1–2 and parallels), which, according to the Gospel accounts, were not understood by his disciples (Mark. 9:31 f., etc.). Nor were the disciples able to understand these predictions because it was expected of the Davidic Messiah that he would "establish the kingdom of His people" (cf. chap. X). It is in this context also that we understand the petition of James and John, the sons of Zebedee, who said to Jesus: "Grant us to sit, one at your right hand and one at your left, in your glory" (Mark 10:35–37; cf. Matt. 20:20 f.). In other words, they want the best governmental posts in the kingdom of God. An analogy of the initial messianic enthusiasm in the synagogue of Nazareth, which turned into hate when it was disappointed, is also provided by the triumphal entry of Jesus into Jerusalem which ended on the Cross of Golgotha. Jesus was received in Jerusalem with the cry, "Hosanna to the Son of David!" (Matt. 21:9 and parallels). What this meant emerges with all the clarity that could be desired in Mark 11:10 "Blessed be the kingdom of our father David that is coming! Hosanna in the highest!" Hosanna is a transliteration of the Hebrew word, *hoshia 'na*, meaning "Save, now!" It is therefore a challenge to the messianic Son of David finally to reveal himself in power and glory. And the same people who had set their hope in him now loudly demanded his crucifixion when they were disappointed and Jesus did not prove himself to be the Davidic messianic commander-in-chief, the expectation of whom is documented in the Qumrân texts (cf. chap. X; Matt. 27:23 and parallels).

A great many parallels to the conceptions in the Qumrân texts and the related pseudepigrapha are also to be found in the so-called apocalyptic discourses of Jesus. Here we shall refer only to the most obvious of them. In Enoch 99:4 we read: "In those days the nations will be in commotion and the generations will rise up on the day of destruction", or 100:2: ". . . from morning till evening will they kill each other." And also according to Matt. 24:7, "nation will rise against nation" (Mark 13:8; Luke 21:10). Likewise the other motifs of Jesus' apocalyptic discourses, such as hunger, earthquakes, pestilence, extreme injustice on earth, uncommon hardship for those with child and those who give suck, are unusually frequent in the pseudepigrapha associated with the Qumrân sphere together with similar descriptions in the Old Testament prophets. In Matt. 24:8 and Mark 13:8 this time is called a time of sufferings. In the later rabbinical texts the term "messianic sufferings" is then applied concretely to the time of woe which precedes the messianic time of salvation. Particularly noteworthy also in connection with the Qumrân texts is the saying of Jesus concerning false prophets and false messiahs: "If they say to you, 'Lo, he is in the wilderness', do not go out" (Matt. 24:26). According to the desert theology of the Qumrân people, the messianic salvation was to be first revealed in the wilderness (cf. chap. VI,2). And according to the War Scroll 1:3, the eschatological war was to begin "when the exiles of the sons of light return from the wilderness of the peoples to encamp in the wilderness of Jerusalem."

The Book of Jubilees 5:1 f. and the angelological portion of the Book of Enoch attribute the evil in the world and the sins largely to the fallen angels and their seductive arts. The Manual of Discipline 3:13–15 also presents the view that "in the hand of the angel of darkness [and his forces] is all dominion over the sinners" and that this same angel of darkness is also responsible for the sins of the righteous. But this will continue only until the "appointed time of God's visitation". Then the powers of darkness and of sin, that is, no doubt, the demons, will be stripped of power once and for all. This is the sense in which Jesus' driving out of demons is also to be understood. The demons no longer have any power to exist. The adherents of the messianic movement would doubtless have understood this to mean that now the dominion of the demons had ceased and therefore that the expected time of salvation had begun. Thus we read in Matt. 12:23: "And all the people were amazed, and said, 'Can this be the Son of David?' " Speaking to the Pharisees, who declared that he drove out demons by the power of Beelzebub, the prince of demons (Matt. 12:22–9; Mark 3:22–7; Luke 11:14–20), Jesus said by way of comparison: "How can one enter a strong man's house and plunder his goods, unless he first binds the strong man?" It may be that here he is alluding to that conception in the pseudepigrapha, according to which the devil was "bound hand and foot" in order "to be cast into the pit of fire on the day of the great judgment" (Enoch 10:4,6).

The action of that apostle who cut off the ear of a slave of the high priest at the arrest of Jesus (Matt. 26:51–3 and parallels) should similarly be understood in the context of the eschatological expectations of the Qumrân sphere. Jesus repudiated this use of force and, according to Matt. 26:53, he is reported to have said that he could draw upon the support of twelve legions of angels if he attached any value to such procedure. Up to the time of the arrest, the apostles and disciples thought that in any military contest they would be the stronger. In the War Scroll and the Hymn Scroll we find documented the conception that the angels of God would participate and be the decisive factor in the final eschatological war (cf. chap. VIII, 3 ff.). It is possible that Jesus' utterance repudiating the use of force had reference to such a conception.

b) The Message of the Angels to the Shepherds of Bethlehem

According to Luke 2:14, the angels sang in praise to God: "Glory to God in the highest and peace to the men of good will on earth." As a rule this good will is interpreted as an inner disposition of men. Peace on earth is to come to those men who themselves have good will. On the basis of the Qumrân texts this interpretation can now be set aside. What matters here is not the good will, the willingness of men, but the good, elective will of God. The Greek word *eudokia* and the Latin word *voluntas* correspond exactly to the Hebrew word *rashon*, whose meaning in the time of Jesus is well known from the Qumrân texts. The term *bechire rashon*, "elect of [God's] good pleasure", in the Manual of Discipline 8,6, corresponds exactly with the term *bechire'el*, "elect of God" in the fragmentary Commentary on Micah from Cave I. In the Hymn Scroll 4:33 it is stated, strongly reminiscent of Luke 2:14, that "the abundance of his mercy" will be "upon all the sons of his good pleasure (*bene reshono*)." Similarly 11:9: "And thy mercy is for all the sons of thy good pleasure." Conversely, the man who is without the *rashon* of God, without the electing good pleasure of God, the man who depends upon himself is utterly powerless: "I am dust and ashes. What can I plan, if thou art unwilling, and what can I think up without thy good pleasure?" (10:5-7).

The man who is touched by divine good pleasure, the chosen one, then also does the will of God for his part. In the Manual of Discipline 5:1,10 we read that God in his good pleasure has laid down laws, and when men keep them they walk in his good pleasure. Hence, if we read the message of the angels in the usage of the Qumrân texts, there can be only one possible interpretation: Peace to the men on earth who are touched by God's electing grace, who have his good pleasure and therefore live to his good pleasure.

c) The Poor in Spirit

For a long time one of the undecided questions of exegesis has been whether to give preference to the phrase of Matt. 5:3, "Blessed are the poor in spirit" or to that of Luke: 6:20, "Blessed are the poor." On the basis of the Qumrân texts it would appear that definite precedence is to be given to the text of Matthew. Professor Stauffer's opinion that the cycle of the Gospel of Matthew "must in many respects have been very close to the spirit of Qumrân" appears to be quite justified.

Who then is meant by the "poor" or the "poor in spirit"? What is the meaning here of the word "spirit"? In the Hebrew or Aramaic original of the Sermon on the Mount the word *ruach* or *rucha* may have been used for "spirit". But *ruach* means not only "wind, breath, spirit", but also "will". Here we need refer only to Exod. 35:21 and Ps. 51:12. Exod. 35:21: "And they came, every one whose heart stirred him, and every one whose spirit [*ruach*, here in the sense of voluntrary agreement] moved him, and brought the Lord's offering to be used for the tent of meeting". Ps. 51:12: "Restore to me the joy of thy salvation, and uphold me with a willing spirit [*ruach* in the same sense as above]". The "poor in spirit" are not therefore "the great mass of little and despised people", nor the proletarians, nor the uneducated *'am ha'ares*, of whom Hillel the Pharisee said a generation before Jesus that they could not be pious because of their ignorance (Sayings of the Fathers II,5), but rather the "voluntarily poor" and those who were willing to be poor even though outwardly they were still in possession of wealth. Poverty in spirit is therefore not an economic concept but a state of grace. The poor in spirit have seen through and overcome the enticements of riches. They are not willing to live in sin for the sake of wealth, but rather are willing, if it is necessary, to sacrifice their riches for the greater and higher goal of the kingdom of God. The poor in spirit are neither paupers nor simpletons but rather according to Isaiah 66:2, they are to be equated with the pious and the obedient to God's word. And this concept of the poor we meet with also in the Qumrân texts. The community called itself a "congregation of the poor" and the members described themselves as "the poor of the Spirit", "the poor of grace", and "poor servants of thy [i.e. God's] redemption" (cf. chap. IX,1,b).

As in the case of the Qumrân Essenes, this ideal of poverty may have had an eschatological character for Jesus too, as is indicated by his use of Isa. 61:1 (cf. chap. XI,2,a). Just as the Qumrân Essenes saw in wealth the temptation to worldliness and the secular attitude as such, so Jesus too regarded it as the strongest of all temptations. This is the sense in which we must understand his saying: "No one can serve two masters. . . . You cannot serve God and mammon" (Matt. 6:24; Luke 16:13). Here also belongs the parable of the unjust steward, Luke 16:1–8, which is an ironical paraphrase of the this-worldly attitude, and ends with the point that the children of this world— in Qumrân terminology they would be called "sons of darkness"—are in their own generation, i.e., as long as this sinful world lasts wiser than the children of light. According to the War Scroll 1:1, however, the dominion of the sons of darkness will be broken by the sons of light at the beginning of the eschatological age. We are reminded of the phrase "mammon of unrighteousness" or "unrighteous mammon" by a similar formula in the Manual of Discipline 10:19, which speaks of *hon ḥamas*, "wealth of injustice, sinful wealth". With this mammon one must, according to Luke 16:9, make friends and not be striving to increase it in dishonest ways (Luke 16:11).

d) *The Messiah, Son and Lord of David*

The Qumrân texts also help us to understand Jesus' controversy with the Pharisaic scribes over the messianic interpretation of Psalm 110:1 (Matt. 22:41–5; Mark 12: 35–7; Luke 20:41–4). Jesus points out the difficulty that the Messiah is to be at once the son and the lord of David. The political, popular hope of the Messiah was connected with the restoration of the Davidic kingdom. The scion of David, the Davidic prince was to establish the kingdom of God. The term "son of David" signifies the same as a new David. The Messianic Florilegium from Cave IV, however, interprets the prophecy of Nathan to David (II Sam. 7:11–14) as meaning that the messianic scion of David of the last days will be the one of whom God said, "I will be his father, and he shall be my son" (cf. chap. X). The messianic son of David was therefore to be identical with the pre-existent Son of God. Thus the question which caused difficulty for Pharisaism is readily understood when we understand the particular presuppositions of the Qumrân doctrine of the Messiah. Perhaps the voice from heaven which said of Jesus after his baptism in the Jordan: "This is my beloved Son, with whom I am well pleased" (Matt. 3:17; Mark 1:11; Luke 3:22) belongs in this context too.

e) Healing by Laying on of Hands

Among the specific things which the practice of Jesus had in common with the Qumrân texts is that of healing by the laying on of hands, which, apart from the New Testament, is mentioned only in the Aramaic Genesis Apocryphon of Qumrân. There we read in 20:21 f.: "And he bade me to come to pray for the king and lay my hands upon him", and 20:29: "I laid my hands upon his head and the affliction left him and the evil spirit fled out of him shrieking." With this may be compared, for example, Luke 13:11–13: "And there was a woman who had a spirit of infirmity for eighteen years; she was bent over and could not fully straighten herself. And when Jesus saw her, he called her and said to her, 'Woman, you are freed from your infirmity'. And he laid his hands upon her, and immediately she was made straight, and she praised God". (David Flusser, "Healing Through the Laying on of Hands in a Dead Sea Scroll", *Israel Exploration Journal* 7 (1957), pp. 107 ff.)

f) The Last Supper

The Last Supper reminds us in many ways of the ritual communal meal of the Essenes (cf. chap. VIII,3,a). At the common meal of the Essenes the presiding priest "first stretches out his hand in order first to bless the bread and wine" Manual of Discipline 6:4–6). This is to be compared with Matt. 26:26: "Now as they were eating, Jesus took bread, and blessed, and broke it. . . . And he took the cup and when he had given thanks. . . ." The external similarity is indeed very striking. But there is an essential difference even in the disposition of the two meals. Jesus was not a priest and yet he presided at the meal. But, what is more, the words of institution at the Last Supper went far beyond the bounds of the Essenes' meal.

The Qumrân texts may also be of critical importance for the dating of the Last Supper. Unlike the rest of Judaism, the Qumrân Essenes employed a solar calendar of fifty-two weeks with a total of three hundred and sixty-four days (cf. chap. VIII,3,d). Therefore, if we were to assume that Jesus celebrated his Last Supper on the eve of the Passover according to the Qumrân calendar, but that the dates of the arrest, trial, and death on the Cross are given in accordance with the Pharisaic calendar, the chronological differences between the Synoptic account and the Gospel of John could be resolved in this way. According to Matt. 26:17; Mark 14:12; Luke 22:7, the Last Supper took place as a paschal meal on the evening of Nisan 14. According to John 19:14, however, the trial before Pilate took place on "the day of Preparation, about the sixth hour", likewise in Nisan 14. Thus the Last Supper must already have taken place on the evening of Nisan 13, and therefore could not have been a paschal meal; this, however, contradicts the account of the Synoptics. But if Jesus celebrated his Last Supper according to the Qumrân Essene calendar, according to which the feast days must always fall on the same day of the month and the week, then the eve of the Passover, on which the paschal lamb was eaten, would always be a Tuesday. The trial before Pilate and the crucifixion could then have taken place on the day of Preparation of the official calendar. Thus there would also have been sufficient time for the arrest and the trial. But this argument, attractive as it is, is not convincing. It overlooks the fact that not a single word of Jesus with regard to the calendar question has been handed down to us. Whereas for the Qumrân people it was an essential and critical problem which separated people from one another, it did not interest Jesus at all. The Qumrân Essenes shunned the temple cult mainly because of their calendar calculations, but Jesus went to the temple more than once. Therefore we must not attempt to solve the chronology of the Last Supper by the Qumrân calendar alone, for there is no sure indication that Jesus and his disciples recognized this calendar.

g) Love of Neighbour and Hatred of Enemies

In Matthew 5:43-4 we read: "You have heard that it was said, 'You shall love your neighbour and hate your enemy.' But I say to you, Love your enemies and pray for those who persecute you." The first part of this saying of Jesus comes from the Old Testament. In Lev. 19:18 love of one's neighbour is expressly and clearly commanded and in 19:34 this precept is also applied specifically to the stranger. The great Pharisee, Hillel, who lived about a generation before Jesus, saw in this commandment the whole law, entire, and said that all the rest is explanation (Shabbat 31 a). But of the second part of Jesus' saying, a commandment to hate one's enemies, there is no proof either in the Old Testament itself or in the literature of the Jewish tradition. Who then were the listeners to Jesus who would have heard that one must hate one's enemy? The Qumrân texts give the answer. There is hardly one of the Dead Sea Scrolls in which this idea is not more or less clearly enunciated. Thus in the Manual of Discipline, for example, we read: "1:4 [It is the duty of the member of the community] to love all whom he [i.e., God] has chosen and hate all whom he has rejected. . . . 1:10, to hate all the sons of darkness, each according to his sinfulness in the vengeance of God. . . . 2:4 f., and the Levites shall curse all men of the lot of Belial and shall answer and say, Accursed are you. . . . 8:6 [It is the task] of the elect of [divine] good pleasure to atone for the earth and requite the wicked. . . . 9:21 f. These are the regulations for the instructor in these times, for his love and for his hate, [which is] an eternal hate with a willingness to cut himself off from all men of corruption." As the Qumrân literature clearly indicates, this hatred of one's enemies had an eschatological character. It is inseparably bound up with the idea of an eschatological war of vengeance, the expectation of which is confirmed not only by the Qumrân texts themselves but also by the exhortations of the Book of Enoch (cf. chap. IX,2,a). The absence of a commandment to hate one's enemies in Pharisaic and Sadducaic Judaism and its frequent occurrence in the Qumrân literature indicates that the Qumrân community and the adherents and the hearers of Jesus sprang from the same milieu. The commandment to love one's enemies, however, shows how far beyond it was the preaching of

Jesus. The idea of a war of vengeance itself was also emphatically rejected by Jesus (Matt. 26:52).

h) Important Differences

As the reversal of the commandment to hate one's enemies into a commandment to love them shows, the milieu of Jesus and the milieu of the Qumrân texts do belong in the same broad framework of the messianic movement, but Jesus himself clearly dissociated himself in many things from his Qumrân Essene predecessors and contemporaries. One of the most important contrasts is probably the completely different evaluation of the Torah. The Qumrân Essenes were by and large even more observant of the law than the Pharisees, but the attitude of Jesus himself towards the Mosaic law was extremely free. Jesus' concept of the fulfilment of the law (Matt. 5:17) and that of the Qumrân people were two completely different things. While the Qumrân Essenes were very rigorous and while they laid great stress upon the strictest purity and ritual precision, Jesus proclaimed that it is not that which goes into the body that defiles a man, but only that which comes out of a man (Mark 7:14–20). The Qumrân Essenes observed the sabbath even more strictly than the Pharisees. Even their predecessors, the *Hasidim rishonim*, rejected fighting on the sabbath, and according to the Damascus Document 11:16 f. the Qumrân Essenes prohibited even the saving of life on the sabbath if any instrument was required to do this (cf. chaps. VI,2; XII). But Jesus without any hesitation quite openly healed a man with a withered hand on the sabbath (Matt. 12:9–13 and parallels). Since there was no danger to life in this instance and therefore the healing might have been postponed until after the sabbath, this enraged the Pharisees, who, according to Shabbat XXII,6, were forbidden even to set a broken bone on the sabbath. If Jesus exasperated even the liberal-conservative Pharisees in this way, how much more would he have offended the Qumrân people who were Torah-fanatics? For Jesus the law is no longer the sole way to a life that is pleasing to God. It is here that an immovable line of demarcation runs between the New Testament and Judaism, whether it be Pharisaic or Essene. A saying like "The Son of man is lord of the sabbath" (Matt. 12:8) would have shocked the Qumrân Essenes even more than the Pharisees. And the plucking of ears of grain on the sabbath (Matt. 12:1–7 and parallels) would have been for them a greater challenge than it was for the Pharisees. According to Mark 2:27, Jesus said in the course of a controversy with the Pharisees on the sabbath problem: "The sabbath was made for man, not man for the sabbath." But this altogether anti-Essene statement is still in line with Pharisaic reasoning. About the middle of the second century after Christ the Tannaite rabbi, Jonathan bar Joseph, made a very similar statement: "The sabbath is holy for you (Exod. 31:14). It is committed into your hands and you are not committed into its hands" (Yoma 85 b).

Whereas the Qumrân Essenes withdrew themselves from all other men, because they "must not engage in any controversy with the men of corruption, but rather conceal the counsel of the Torah in the midst of sinners" (Manual of Discipline 9:16 f.) and were not allowed to accept either food or drink from any outsiders (Manual of Discipline 5:16 f.), Jesus was not only seen in the houses of Pharisees but he and his disciples were even the guests of "publicans and sinners" (Luke 7:34, 36–9), nor did Jesus hesitate to allow his feet to be washed by an openly sinful woman. What a difference between the ideals of the Qumrân fellowship and the practice of Jesus! If John the Baptist had already broken through the sectarian character of Qumrân Essene Judaism and turned to all Israel with his message (cf. chap. XI,1), Jesus and his circle were even more broad-minded. There is actually not a trace of the sectarian narrowness and group-snobbery of the Qumrân people in Jesus.

In line with this is also the view of all four evangelists that the teaching of Jesus, at least in essence, is not a secret doctrine, which may be made known only to a narrow circle of the elect, but one which concerns all men. If it is given only to a small circle of the blessed to know the "secrets of the kingdom of God" (Matt. 13:11; Mark 4:11; 8:10), they are nevertheless proclaimed to all. Whereas the Qumrân people were intent upon the strictest anonymity in their texts and thus made it so difficult for us to-day to identify persons like the Wicked Priest, the Man of Lies, or the Teacher of Righteousness with personalities in Jewish history, there are no such difficulties in understanding the New Testament. All persons are referred to by name. There are no more pseudonyms here as may be found in an underground movement. The Qumrân people also avoided precise time indications, whereas Luke 3:1 f., is a model of the most exact chronology. A further important difference between Qumrân and Jesus that must be mentioned is the fact that Jesus in no way rejected the temple as a place of sacrifice, as did the Qumrân Essenes. Jesus drove the money-changers and traders out of the temple (Matt. 21:12 f.; Mark 11:15–17; Luke 19:45 f.; John 2:14–16); but this can only mean that keeping the sanctuary pure was of importance to him.

All in all, and based on the tradition of his person transmitted by the evangelists—the distinction between the historical Jesus and the Jesus Christ of the proclamation being irrelevant in this context—it can be said of the relation of Jesus to the Qumrân Essenes, that though he is related to them by a common milieu, his teaching and his person lead us far beyond it.

3. THE PRIMITIVE CHURCH AT JERUSALEM
AND THE QUMRÂN TEXTS

As communal ownership was practiced in Essene circles (cf. chap. VIII,2,a), so it was also known and propagated in the primitive church of Jerusalem. In Acts 2:44 f., we read: "And all who believed were together and had all things in common; and they sold their possessions and goods and distributed them to all, as any had need" (refer also to Acts 4:34–7). Especially interesting in this connection is the story of Ananias and Sapphira (Acts 5:1–11), whose deceit with respect to the voluntary surrender of their possessions was punished with death by a divine judgment from heaven. The Qumrân community also placed this and similar offences under the sanction of punishment. Thus we read in the Manual of Discipline 6:24 f.: "If there is any among them who makes false declarations about his wealth and the matter comes to light, he shall be excluded from the purity of the full members for a year." The position of Peter in the story of Ananias and Sapphira is strongly reminiscent of the office mentioned in Man. Dis. 6:12–20, Dam. Doc. 9: 17–22, and elsewhere, which is given the title *mevaqqer*, which is perhaps best translated as supervisor or overseer. Also according to the Manual of Discipline 6:20, the *mevaqqer* receives into custody the property of persons newly admitted to the community. The Christian office of bishop may have had an antecedent in the office of the *mevaqqer.*

One of the most important acts of the primitive church was the communal breaking of bread (Acts 2:42), and the ritual meal of the Essenes should probably be associated with this, but it was not comparable with it in all respects (cf. chap. VIII,3,a). In both instances the table fellowship grew out of the spirit of community ownership (Acts 2:44 f.); nevertheless the difference between the meal of the primitive church and that of the Essenes lies in the meaning that was given to it by Jesus (cf. chap. XI,2,f.). In other respects, too, the sociological structure based on community which was characteristic of both the New Testament community and that of the Essenes did not produce the same results in both cases. The New Testament makes no mention of novices or of communal life and labour. It was not until later that monasticism introduced these things.

Besides the office of *mevaqqer* and community of goods, the primitive Christian church was acquainted with still other institutions and nomenclature which we know from the Qumrân texts. The full members of the Qumrân community called themselves *rabbim*, "the many, the numerous"; and in Acts 6:2,5; 15:12,30 a Christian congregation is called *to plethos*, "the multitude". Following the number of twelve apostles, the primitive church had a committee of twelve at the head of the congregation (Acts 6:2). When Judas was excluded from the number of the twelve, his place had to be filled by the selection of Matthias to the office of apostle (Acts 1:15–26). This reminds us of a regulation in the Manual of Discipline 8:1 which reads: "In the council of the community there are twelve men and three priests." Some expositors count the three priests among the twelve in this passage, but such an interpretation does not appear to be absolutely necessary. Even from a literal reading of this passage it must be viewed as an important parallel to the corresponding practice in the primitive church. The point is that the primitive church, in contrast to the Qumrân community, was not led by priests, and therefore the three priests were no longer of any importance to the primitive church. Alongside the office of apostle there was in the primitive church the office of the *presbyteroi,* the "elders" (Acts 11:30; 15:2–22). With these may be compared the "heads of the fathers of the community" mentioned in the Book of Rules and the War Scroll (cf. chap. VIII,2,a) and the "elders" mentioned in the Manual of Discipline 6:8. In Acts 9:13; 26:10 (cf. Rom. 15:25,31) the members of the Christian church are called "saints". The Qumrân people also called themselves "men of holiness" (Manual of Discipline 5:13; Dam. Doc. 20:2), and they called their community "a holy house for Israel and a most holy congregation for Aaron" (Manual of Discipline 8:5 f.).

Among the Qumrân Essenes and in the primitive church of Jerusalem the same messianic passages from the Old Testament were frequently cited. Naturally, in the primitive church, in contrast to Qumrân, they were applied to Jesus as the Christ. In Acts 2:30 there is an allusion to II Sam. 7:12 f., a passage which is also cited in the Messianic Florilegium from Cave IV (cf. chap. I,3 a,ii). In his address to the people, Peter applied to Jesus (Acts 3:22) the prophecy concerning the coming prophet in Deut. 18:15,18 who will be like Moses. This passage is also found in the collection of Messianic Testimonies from Cave IV, where it points to the expected messianic prophet, and thus very probably to the Teacher of Righteousness (cf. chap. X). When Peter and the apostles were called a second time to account for preaching contrary to the prohibition of the council, Peter replied, according to Acts 5:31: "God exalted him [Jesus] at his right hand as Prince (*archegos*) and Saviour (*soter*)". The Greek word *archegos* corresponds to the Hebrew word *naśi*, "prince", which in the Qumrân texts, with reference to Ezek. 34:24; 37:25, is a designation for the Davidic Messiah (cf. chap. X). Just as the Jesus who has been raised to be the "Prince" is called Saviour by Peter, so, according to the Messianic Florilegium from Cave IV, the messianic "scion of David" (cf. chap. X) shall "save Israel" in the last days. Also the passage Amos 9:11, "I will raise up the booth of David that is fallen", mentioned in the Messianic Florilegium from Cave IV and the Damascus Document 7:16, appears again in Acts 15:16.

Like the Qumrân Essenes, the primitive Christian church also believed that it was living in a "new covenant" (cf. chap. IX,1,a). But for the Qumrân Essenes this term meant no more than a "renewed covenant", for the community was still awaiting the messianic redemption. For the primitive church, however, an intrinsically new covenant had come, a covenant which was more than a renewal of the old covenant because for it the messianic Redeemer had already come. Thus we read: "For this is my blood of the new covenant, which is poured out for many for the forgiveness of sins" (Matt. 26:28 and parallels). The essential difference between the Qumrân community and early Christianity consisted therefore in the fact that the former lived in expectation of the imminent coming of the Messiah, whereas the latter proclaimed its fulfilment (e.g., Acts 2:22–4; 10:40–2).

How did it come about that the primitive church was so strongly influenced by elements which are also documented among the Qumrân Essenes? Both the followers of Jesus and the Qumrân Essenes belonged to the messianic movement. But beyond this it is quite conceivable that many members of the primitive church had been Essenes before they came to believe in Jesus as the Christ. In Acts 6:7 it is expressly stated that a great many of the priests accepted the faith. Here it is more likely that we should think of the Saddoqitic priests of the Qumrân Essenes (cf. chaps. VI,1,a; VII) rather than the Sadducaic priests, who, because of the Sadducaic denial of the resurrection (Acts 23:8; Matt. 22:23–32; Josephus, *Bellum* 2,8,14), were also unable to believe in the resurrection of Jesus. In contrast to the Qumrân Essenes' tendency towards segregation, the primitive church of Jerusalem was open to everyone. In Acts 15:5 there is specific mention of Pharisees who accepted the faith. Moreover, the Council of Jerusalem (A.D. 49–50) decided that Gentiles might be received into the church of Christ without first being circumcized (Acts 15:10,19; Gal. 2:9), an idea which would have been unthinkable in the Qumrân sphere. Nor were the members of the primitive church as critical of the temple as were the Qumrân Essenes (cf. chap. VIII,3,c), but "resorted with one accord to the temple" (Acts 2:46; cf. 3:1,11). Here they followed a practice of Jesus himself (cf. chap. XI,2,h).

4. THE RELATION OF THE QUMRÂN TEXTS TO THE GOSPEL OF JOHN AND THE JOHANNINE LETTERS

The Gospel of John and the Johannine letters can be understood in the broadest sense of the word as a coming to grips (*Auseinandersetzung*) with the theological presuppositions of the Qumrân Essenes. One frequently has the impression that a Christology for Essenes is being presented here. Thus one of the most important results of Qumrân research has been to prove the Jewish origin of the Gospel of John conclusively. This is not to deny or to minimize the fact that there was also a strong Hellenistic influence. Even in the Qumrân texts themselves there are traces of such influence (cf. chap. VIII,3,h, beginning). However, neither the dualistic view of the world in general nor the Johannine light-darkness doctrine in particular are to be traced back exclusively to Hellenistic influence. The comparison of John 1:3 and the Manual of Discipline 11:11 should be sufficient to illustrate the close relationship between Qumrân and the Gospel of John. John 1:3: "All things were made through the Logos, and without him was not anything made that was made." Manual of Discipline 11:11; "By his [i.e. God's] knowledge everything came into being; everything that is he directs according to his plan. Except through him nothing is wrought." But here, as everywhere else, we can already see the fundamental difference between the Qumrân teachings and Christianity. The one who is the "God of knowledge" in the Manual of Discipline is for John's Gospel the Logos Christ.

According to the teaching of the Qumrân Essenes, God "created the spirit of light and of darkness and upon them founded every work" (Manual of Discipline 3:25; cf. chap. VIII,3,f, beginning). The same dualism prevails in the Gospel of John and the Johannine letters. But whereas for the Manual of Discipline 4:19 the "appointed time of his visitation", when God will root out evil once and for all, still lies in the future, for John 1:5 "the light shines in the darkness" which cannot overcome it, and according to I John 2:8: "the darkness is passing away and the true light is already shining." For the author of the Gospel of John, therefore, the battle between light and darkness has already been decided in principle, since for him Jesus was the "light of the world" (John 8:12).

The similarities in style between the Gospel of John and the Qumrân texts are so striking that a close connection cannot be denied. In the Manual of Discipline 3:20 f., we read that the sons of righteousness *"walk in the ways of light"*, whereas the sons of error *"walk in the ways of darkness."* This is to be compared with John 8:12: "I am the light of the world; he who follows me *will not walk in darkness*, but will have the light of life;" or John 12:35: *"Walk* while you have the *light*, lest the darkness overtake you; he who *walks in the darkness* does not know where he goes" (cf. I John 1:5–7). Just as the Manual of Discipline 1:9 f. speaks of the sons of light and the sons of darkness, John 12:36 also speaks of the "sons of light" (cf. Luke 16:8). The pairs of opposites, light-darkness, truth-perversity, evil, error and vice versa are used both in the Johannine writings and the Qumrân texts. Thus, for example, we read in John 3:19–21: "And this is the judgment, that the light has come into the world, and men loved darkness rather than the light, because their deeds were evil. For every one who does evil hates the light. . . . But he who does what is true comes to the light." Compare this with the Manual of Discipline 3:18,25, which speaks of the "spirits of truth and of perversity" and in the second instance, of "spirits of light and of darkness." John 14:16 f.; 16:13 speaks of a special comforter, the "Spirit of truth", who will teach all truth. So we read also in the Manual of Discipline 4:21: "He [i.e. God] sprinkles upon him the spirit of truth like purifying water [to cleanse him] from all abominations of the lie." The view of John 3:20 f.; that he who does evil hates the light, but he who does the truth comes to the light, finds its parallel in the Manual of Discipline 4:24: "According to each man's share of possession in truth and righteousness, he hates error; and according to his inheritance in the lot of error, he does evil in it and abhors the truth." If John 3:21 characterizes right conduct as "doing the truth", this term is already documented in the Manual of Discipline 8:2.

According to the Qumrân Essenes' view, the spirits of light and of darkness are subject to God (cf. chap. VIII 3,f.); but for I John 1:5 "God [himself] is light and in him is no darkness at all." In the Gospel of John, Christ is also the light of the world (John 8:12; 9:5). In the Qumrân texts and in the Johannine literature there are two leaders of light and darkness. For the Qumrân Essenes both are created instruments of God (Manual of Discipline 3:25). But since for the author of the Gospel of John, Christ himself is the light, the Johannine view differs from that of the Qumrân Essenes, since for them the angel of light is only a creature of God. According to the view of the Qumrân texts, the angel of light stands against the angel of darkness; in the Gospel of John, Christ stands against the "prince of this world" (John 12:31; 14:30; 16:11).

These references may suffice to justify the supposition made at the beginning of this section to the effect that in the Johannine literature we have a Christian addressing himself to Essene teachings. A number of theories have already been put forward in an attempt to explain this close connection, but since all of them are still too uncertain at the present stage of investigation, we shall not discuss them in this brief summary.

5. PAUL AND THE QUMRÂN TEXTS

The teachings of the apostle Paul also show many parallels to those of the Qumrân Essenes. As a Pharisee he may have become familiar with most of the views, which he later championed, through polemical discussion with the adherents of the various messianic groups. When he himself became a Christian he learned them first-hand and many of their elements he made his own. Perhaps the most obvious common element in the theology of Paul and the Qumrân texts is their deep consciousness of sin. By himself man can do nothing; only God can justify him. But the Pharisaism from which Paul came trusted in works as the fulfilling of the law. According to Romans 3:23 f., however, all [i.e., both Jews and Gentiles] have sinned and fell short of the glory of God; they are justified by his grace as a gift, through the redemption which is in Christ Jesus." This one example of Pauline consciousness of sin and the Pauline doctrine of justification is sufficient for our purpose, since it is paradigmatic. Similarly we read in the Hymn Scroll 4:30 f., that man "is in sin from the womb and in sinful revolt to old age. I have known that righteousness is not with man and perfect conduct is not with the son of man; [but] with the Most High God are all works of righteousness." Here again the external similarity is striking, but what obtained elsewhere applies quite especially to Paul; the difference from the Qumrân texts consists in faith in Jesus as the Christ. This difference becomes very clear if we compare Paul's interpretation of Hab. 2:4 with that of the author of the Habakkuk Commentary. Paul holds that works according to the law of the Torah are of no account; the one thing, for him, that is important is faith in Jesus, through whom believing Gentiles can participate in the faith of Abraham. In one such connection he says, "Now it is evident that no man is justified before God by the law; for 'He who through faith is righteous shall live" (Gal. 3:11; Hab. 2:4). The Habakkuk Commentary 8:1–3 interprets the same passage in Habakkuk as follows: "This refers to all those of the house of Judah who live according to the Torah, whom God will rescue from the place of judgment because of their labour and their faith in the Teacher of Righteousness." The author of the Habakkuk Commentary also requires faith in the Teacher of Righteousness, that is, in his message; but it is not a justifying faith as in the theology of Paul. For him, faith in the Teacher presupposes works of the Torah, in other words, works in fulfilment of the law according to the Qumrân community's particular interpretation of the law. Along with faith in the Teacher of Righteousness, there is still another factor of equal value, namely, the "labour" of the sectarians of Qumrân, which probably means the rigorously ascetic and strictly legalistic life of the Qumrân Essenes. For the author of the Habakkuk Commentary, works of the Torah are prerequisites for faith in the Teacher of Righteousness; for Paul they stand in the way of faith in Jesus.

The light-darkness dualism, which plays a large role in the Johannine writings, is also characteristic of the theology of Paul (cf. chap. VIII,3,f.). Thus we read in Rom. 13:12: "Let us then cast off the works of darkness and put on the armour of light," In Acts 26:18 Paul speaks of turning away from darkness to light, which is the equivalent of turning away from the power of Satan to God (cf. II Cor. 6:14 f.). A clear parallel to the Manual of Discipline 4:2–14 is presented in the catalogue of sins and merits in

Gal. 5:19–26: "Now the works of the flesh are plain: immorality, impurity, licentiousness, idolatry, sorcery, enmity, strife, jealousy, anger, selfishness, dissension, party spirit, envy, drunkenness, carousing, and the like. . . . But the fruit of the Spirit is love, joy, peace, patience, kindness, goodness, faithfulness, gentleness, self-control." And in the Manual of Discipline 4:2–14 we read: "These are their ways on earth. [It is the task of the spirit of truth] to enlighten the heart of man and to make straight before him all the paths of righteousness and truth, and to make his heart to be in dread of the judgments of God: a spirit of humility, forbearance, abundant love, and eternal goodness, of understanding, insight, and true wisdom, which trusts in all the works of God and leans upon the abundance of his grace; a spirit of knowledge of all creative thought [of God?] and zeal for all righteous judgments. . . . Signs of the spirit of error are arrogance, slackness of hands in the service of righteousness, wickedness, falsehood, pride, haughtiness, lying and deceit, cruelty, rank dissimulation, impatience, unusual folly, wanton zeal for abominable works in the spirit of fornication, impure ways in impure worship, a blasphemous tongue, blindness of eyes, dullness of ears, stiffness of neck, and hardness of heart, so that a man walks in all the ways of darkness and evil cunning."

6. THE EPISTLE TO THE HEBREWS
AND THE QUMRÂN TEXTS

The themes of the Epistle to the Hebrews make it clear that it was addressed to Jewish Christians from the circles of the Qumrân Essenes or Jews whose doctrine of the Messiah was similar to that of the Qumrân Essenes. The letter opens with the remark that God originally spoke to the fathers through the prophets, but then appointed the Son as his spokesman (Heb. 1:1-3). The Qumrân texts make it very clear that the Qumrân Essenes expected a messianic prophet to come before the advent of the two Messiahs (cf. chap. X); and, according to the Messianic Testimonies from Cave IV, they identified this messianic prophet with the new prophet who would be like Moses (Deut. 18:15,18). But instead of speaking through the new prophet, God "has in these last days spoken to us by a Son" (Heb. 1:2). Jesus as the Son is therefore at the same time the last prophet. The theme of the third chapter, which establishes the superiority of Jesus over Moses, may also belong in this context.

In conjunction with the establishment of the superiority of Jesus over the prophets, the author of the letter to the Hebrews deals with the superiority of Jesus over the angels. Jesus is more than the angels, for God said to him: "Thou art my Son, to-day I have begotten thee" (Ps. 2:7) and "I will be to him a father, and he shall be to me a son" (II Sam. 7:14; Heb. 1:5). As Jesus by his Sonship stands above the prophets, by this same quality he also stands above the angels. The prophecy in II Sam. 7:14 is applied in the Messianic Florilegium from Cave IV to the expected Davidic Messiah of the last days. But according to the Qumrân texts, the angels of God take part in the eschatological war and are a decisive factor in it, quite independent of the two Messiahs (cf. chaps. VIII, 3,f.; IX, 2,a). There is no mention here of any possible subordination to the Messiahs or to one of them.

The most important theme of the Epistle to the Hebrews, however, is the claim that Jesus, even though he is Davidic, is also a high priest after the order of Melchisedec (7:14-16). The Levitical priesthood of the Aaronites, upon whose pure saddoqiditic line the Qumrân people laid great stress, is subordinated to this priesthood after the order of Melchisedec (7:5–11). The sons of Levi, who themselves receive the tithes, were in Abraham's loins when he gave tithes to Melchisedec. Thus the priesthood of Melchisedec is above the priesthood of Aaron, and if Jesus is a high priest after the order of Melchisedec, he stands above an Aaronitic high priest. Here we have a clear denial of the Qumrân doctrine of the Messiah, in which the high-priestly Aaronite Messiah takes precedence in cultic matters over the Davidic Messiah (cf. chap. X). Thus the writer of the Epistle to the Hebrews was concerned to prove that in Jesus all three messianic aspects of the Qumrân doctrine of the Messiah are united, the prophetic, the Davidic, and the high-priestly. (Yigael Yadin, "The Dead Sea Scroll and the Epistle to the Hebrews", *Scripta Hierosolymitana* IV (1957), pp. 36–55.)

XII

THE QUMRÂN COMMUNITY AND
RABBINISM

SINCE the Qumrân community and Pharisaism have a
common origin in the movement of the *Hasidim rishonim* in
the early Maccabean period (cf. chaps. VI,2; VII) and
since the Qumrân Essenes did not, like early Christianity,
go beyond the general framework of Judaism, there are a
number of elements common to these two groups. The
differences consist essentially in their differing attitudes
toward the near expectation of the Messiah. Because of
their acute eschatological expectation, the Qumrân Essenes
were more tightly organized and more radical than the
Pharisees. Nevertheless, there were even in Pharisaic
circles particular groups, called *havurot*, who laid great
stress on "purity", a concept which was also a decisive
factor in the Qumrân Essene way of life. According to the
Manual of Discipline 6:16 f., the candidate for membership of the Qumrân Essene monastic community who has
been admitted to the novitiate is still not permitted to
"touch the purity of the full members" (cf. chap. VIII,2,a).
According to Tos. Demai 2, it is required of a *haver*, an
"Associate," that is, a member of a *havura*, that he "must
not perform his 'purity' [purifications] in the presence of
the unlearned [in the original, *'am ha'ares*] and must eat
his profane meals in 'purity' ". Even though the word

"purity" does not necessarily mean the same thing in both instances, the same principle is no doubt involved. It may also be possible that the meal mentioned in Tos. Demai 2, which is to be eaten in "purity", had some sort of connection with the communal meal of the Qumrân Essenes (cf. chap. VIII,3,a). Parallel with these, perhaps purely formal, similarities there were also great dissimilarities between the organization of the *havurot* and that of the Qumrân community. For example, a scholar could become a member of a *havura* at once, whereas the rules for admission mentioned in the Manual of Discipline 6:13–23 probably applied to everybody without exception—at least to those who wished to join the monastic centre of the community.

In contrast with Christianity, the Mosaic law retained its validity both for the Pharisees and for the Qumrân Essenes. Their interpretation of this law differed, however. To illustrate that difference we shall mention only their differing interpretation of the sabbath. In the Damascus Document 11:16 f., we read: "If any person falls into a cistern or into a pool on the sabbath, one must not bring him up by means of a ladder, or rope, or any other instrument." Compare this with Yoma 8,6: "Every danger to life overrides the sabbath;" and Yoma 84b (bar) which recommends that one should not be anxious in such case, but rather lend a hand immediately and without scruples. The same spirit pervades the stipulation in Shabbat 18:3, which makes it permissible to help a woman in childbirth and to make use of a midwife on the sabbath. The Pharisaic attitude toward the sabbath is also made very clear in the regulation contained in Shabbat 2:5: "If a man put out the lamp on the sabbath from fear of the Gentiles or of thieves or of an evil spirit, or to suffer one that was sick to sleep, he is not culpable. But if he desires only to spare the lamp or to spare the oil or to spare the wick, he is culpable." Among the Qumrân Essenes, for whom the saving of life on the sabbath was forbidden and who classed all non-Jews as "vain heathen" (War Scroll 9:9; 11:9), the Pharisaic precept, which directed that even the greatest day of rest and holiness, the Day of Atonement, might be desecrated for the sake of a Gentile whose life was in danger, would have been impossible. In Yoma 8:7, however, we read: "If a building fell down upon a man and there is doubt whether he is there or not, or whether he is alive or dead, or whether he is a Gentile or an Israelite, they may clear away the ruin from above him. If they find him alive they may clear it away still more from above him; but if dead, they leave him." The non-Jew was therefore regarded essentially with more kindness by the Pharisees than by the Qumrân Essenes. A view like that of Rabbi Joshua ben Hananiah (beginning of the second century after Christ), according to which the righteous among the nations of the world will have a portion in the world to come (Tos. Sanhedrin 13:2; Sanhedrin 105a), would have been utterly impossible in the circles of the Qumrân community.

The Damascus Document 11:13 simply states: "Let no man help an animal to give birth on the sabbath", whereas in Shabbat 18:3 this precept is restricted to the effect that one may at least give a little help to the dam. These few examples may be sufficient to show that Pharisaism was far less strict than Qumrân Essenism.

But just as the Qumrân Essenes stiffened the law on account of their acute messianic expectation and awaited an eschatological war of vengeance, while the Pharisees' interpretation of the law was more liberal than that of the

Qumrân people, owing to their sceptical attitude toward the messianic groups, so the Pharisees, in contrast to the Qumrân Essenes, developed ethics for dealing with one's neighbour (cf. chap. VII). A concept like that of the Manual of Discipline 1:10 f., that one must "hate all the sons of darkness, each according to his sinfulness in the vengeance of God", was alien to Pharisaism. Thus in Shabbat 31 we find a statement made by the Pharisee Hillel, who lived about a generation before Jesus: "Do not do to your neighbour what you hate to have done to you. This is the whole Torah, entire; all the rest is only explanation." Rabbi Akiba, who lived in the first third of the second century after Christ, is reported, in Genesis Rabbah 24, end, to have said: " 'Thou shalt love thy neighbour as thyself.' This is a very important rule in the Torah. See that you do not say, Inasmuch as I have been despised, my neighbour shall be despised with me; inasmuch as I have been reviled, my neighbour shall be reviled with me. R. Tanchuma said: If you should do this, then know that he whom you despise was created in the image of God."

As these brief comparisons show, Pharisaism avoided the dangers which were inherent in the sectarian attitude of the Qumrân Essenes. Both the Qumrân Essenes and Pharisaism thought of themselves as a penitential movement; but while the former required too much of men, the latter was able to invest the Mosaic law with a new actuality which was conformable with the diaspora of Judaism. The Qumrân Essenes, because of their immediate expectation of the approaching end of the world, were capable of the most extreme religious exertions, but as the end was delayed again and again they probably came to a rather inglorious end in the Jewish-Roman war of A.D. 66–70. The Pharisees, however, reckoned with the reality of this world from the beginning and therefore its continuing existence could not shake them. Pharisaism combined the messianic idea with the idea of election and thus found a meaning and a purpose for Judaism in a world which from a purely external point of view is still in a desperate state.

APPENDIX

I. LITERATURE

(arranged according to year of publication)

1950 A. DUPONT SOMMER, *Aperçus préliminaires sur les Manuscrits de la Mer Morte*, Paris 1950.

1951 PAUL KAHLE, *Die hebräischen Handschriften aus der Höhle*, Stuttgart 1951.

1952 A. DUPONT SOMMER, *The Dead Sea Scrolls*, Oxford and New York 1952. (Translation of the above-mentioned work by the same author.)

HAROLD H. ROWLEY, *The Zadokite Fragments and the Dead Sea Scrolls*, Oxford 1952.

A. M. HABERMANN, *Eda we'edut*, Jerusalem 1952.

HANS BARDTKE, *Die Handschriftenfunde am Toten Meer*, Berlin 1952.

1953 A. DUPONT SOMMER, *Nouveaux Aperçus sur les Manuscrits de la Mer Morte*, Paris 1953.

KARL ELLIGER, *Studien zum Habakukkommentar vom Toten Meer*, Tübingen 1953.

1954 A. DUPONT SOMMER, *The Jewish Sect of Qumrân and the Essenes*, London 1954.
(Translation of the above-mentioned work by the same author).

GEORG MOLIN, *Die Söhne des Lichtes*, Vienna 1954.

GÉZA VERMÈS, *Les Manuscrits du Désert de Juda*, Paris 1954.

A. MICHEL, *Le Maitre de Justice*, Paris 1954.

1955 EDMUND WILSON, *The Scrolls from the Dead Sea*, New York and London 1955.

MILLAR BURROWS, *The 'Dead Sea Scrolls*, New York 1955, London 1956.

ALBERT VINCENT, *Les Manuscrits Hébreux du Désert de Juda*, Paris 1955.

SABATINO MOSCATI, *I Manoscritti ebraici del deserto di Guida*, Rome 1955.

OTTO SCHLIESKE, *Der Schatz von Jericho*, Stuttgart 1955.

HAROLD H. ROWLEY, *The Dead Sea Scrolls and their Significance*, London 1955.

1956 HUGH J. SCHONFIELD, *Secrets of the Dead Sea Scrolls*, London 1956.

CHARLES T. FRITSCH, *The Qumrân Community, Its History and Scrolls*, New York and London 1956.

FREIDRICH NÖTSCHER, *Zur theologischen Terminologie der Qumrântexte*, Bonn 1956.

GEOFFREY GRAYSTONE, *The Dead Sea Scrolls and the Originality of Christ*, London 1956.

EDMUND WILSON, *Die Schriftrollen vom Toten Meer*, Munich 1956. (Translation of the above-mentioned work by the same author.)

JOHN MARCO ALLEGRO, *The Dead Sea Scrolls*, London 1956.

A. DUPONT SOMMER, *Les Esséniens*, in *Evidences* No. 54 ff., January 1956 ff.

H. WILDBERGER, *Die Handschriftenfunde beim Toten Meer und ihre Bedeutung für die Erforschung der heiligen Schrift*, Stuttgart 1956 (Calwer Hefte No. 5).

THEODOR H. GASTER, *The Dead Sea Scriptures*, New York 1956, London 1957.

GÉZA VERMÈS, *Discovery in the Judean Desert, The Dead Sea Scrolls and their Meaning*, New York 1956. (Translation and expansion of the above-mentioned work by the same author.)

WILLIAM SANDFORD LASOR, *Amazing Dead Sea Scrolls and the Christian Faith*, Chicago 1956.

A. POWELL DAVIES, *The Meaning of the Dead Sea Scrolls*, New York 1956, London 1957.

F. F. BRUCE, *Second Thoughts on the Dead Sea Scrolls*, London 1956.

F. F. BRUCE, *The Teacher of Righteousness in the Qumrân Texts*, London 1956.

1957 ETHELBERT STAUFFER, *Jesus und die Wüstengemeinde am Toten Meer*, Stuttgart 1957 (Calwer Hefte No. 9).

MILLAR BURROWS, *Die Schriftrollen vom Toten Meer*, Munich 1957. (Translation of the above-mentioned work by the same author.)

GEORG MOLIN, *Lob Gottes aus der Wüste*, Freiburg and Munich 1957.

KRISTER STENDAHL, *The Scrolls and the New Testament*, New York 1957.

YIGAEL YADIN, *Hammegillot haggenuzot mimmidbar Jehuda*, Jerusalem 1957.

YIGAEL YADIN, *The Message of the Scrolls*, London 1957. (Translation of the above-mentioned work by the same author.)

H. E. DEL MEDICO, *L'Enigme des Manuscrits de la Mer Morte*, Paris 1957.

JEAN DANIÉLOU, *Les Manuscrits de la Mer Morte et les Origines du Christianisme*, Paris 1957.

HAROLD H. ROWLEY, *Jewish Apocalyptic and the Dead Sea Scrolls*, London 1957.

HAROLD H. ROWLEY, *The Scrolls and the New Testament*, London 1957.

HERBERT BRAUN, *Spätjüdisch häretischer und frühchristlicher Radikalismus, Jesus von Nazareth und die essenische Qumrânsekte*, 2 Vols., Tübingen 1957. (Beiträge zur historischen Theologie 24.)

CHRISTOPH BURCHARD, *Bibliographie zu den Handschriften vom Toten Meer*, Berlin 1957. (Beihefte zur Zeitschrift für die alttestamentliche Wissenschaft 76.)

J. T. MILIK, *Dix Ans des Découverts dans le Désert de Juda*. Paris 1957.

CHAIM RABIN, *Qumrân Studies*, London 1957. (Scripta Judaica II.)

JOHN MARCO ALLEGRO, *Die Botschaft vom Toten Meer*,

Frankfurt/Main 1957. (Translation of the above-mentioned work by the same author.)

Ijjunim bimgillot midbar Jehuda, Jerusalem 1957.

J. VAN DER PLOEG, *Vondsten in de Woestijn van Juda*, Utrecht 1957.

F. F. BRUCE, *Die Handschriftenfunde am Toten Meer*, Munich 1957. (Translation of the above-mentioned work by the same author.)

DUNCAN HOWLETT, *The Essenes and Christianity*, New York 1957.

MEIR WALLENSTEIN, *The Nezer and the Submission in Suffering Hymn from the Dead Sea Scrolls*, Istanbul 1957.

A. S. VAN DER WOUDE, *Die messianischen Vorstellungen der Gemeinde von Qumrân*, Assen 1957.

R. E. MURPHY, *The Dead Sea Scrolls and the Bible*, Westminster 1957.

Les Manuscrits de la Mer Morte, Paris 1957

CHARLES F. PFEIFFER, *The Dead Sea Scrolls*, Grand Rapids 1957.

P. WERNBERG MÖLLER, *The Manual of Discipline*, Leiden 1957.

1958 A. POWELL DAVIES, *Der Fund von Qumrân, Die Schriftrollen vom Toten Meer und die Bibel*, Wiesbaden 1958. (Translation of the above-mentioned work by the same author.)

FRANC M. CROSS, *The Ancient Library of Qumran and Modern Biblical Studies*, New York 1958.

MILLAR BURROWS, *More Light on the Dead Sea Scrolls*, New York 1958.

HERBERT HAAG, *Die Handschriftenfunde aus der Wüste Juda*, Bäden bei Zürich 1958. (Biblische Beiträge 15/16.)

HAROLD H. ROWLEY, *The Dead Sea Scrolls from Qumrân*, Southampton 1958.

FREIDRICH NÖTSCHER, *Gotteswege und Menschenwege in der Bibel und in Qumrân*, Bonn 1958.

Aspects of the Dead Sea Scrolls, Jerusalem 1958, (Scripta Hierosolymitana IV).

JEAN CARMIGNAC, *La Règle de la Guerre*, Paris 1958.

2. EDITIONS OF THE TEXT

i. *The Finds of the Bedouins in the year 1947*

a. Published by the American School of Oriental Research

MILLAR BURROWS, *The Dead Sea Scrolls of Saint Mark's Monastery*, Vol. I: *The Isaiah Manuscript and the Habakkuk Commentary*, New Haven, 1950. Vol. II, Fascicle 2: *Plates and Transcriptions of the Manual of Discipline*, New Haven, 1951.

b. Published by scholars of the Hebrew University in Jerusalem

E. L. SUKENIK, *Oṣar hammegillot haggenuzot*, Jerusalem, 1954. (Brief introduction and text of Isaiah Scroll "B", the War Scroll, and the Hymn Scroll.)

YIGAEL YADIN, *Milhemet bene or bibne hosheh*, Jerusalem 1955. (Text of the War Scroll with commentary.)

JACOB LICHT, *Megillat hahodaiot*, Jerusalem 1957. (Text of the Hymn Scroll with commentary.)

NACHMAN AVIGAD–YIGAEL YADIN, *A Genesis Apocryphon*, Jerusalem 1956.

ii. *Finds in Cave I in the excavations of the Spring of 1949*

D. BARTHÉLEMY, O.P. and J. T. MILIK, *Discoveries in the Judaean Desert*, Vol. 1: *Qumrân Cave I*, Oxford 1955.

iii. *Only a few fragments of the texts found in the other caves have so far been published in various scholarly journals. Only the following have appeared in book form:*

KARL GEORG KUHN, *Phylakterien aus Höhle 4 von Qumrân*, Heidelberg 1957. Abhandlungen der Heidelberger Akademie der Wissenschaften, Phil.–hist. Klasse, 1957, 1.

3. PUBLICATIONS OF THE AUTHOR ON THE QUMRÂN TEXTS

"Ein Höhlenfund bei Jericho", *Wort und Wahrheit* 4 (1949), pp. 636–40.

"Die Texte aus der Sektiererhöhle bei Jericho", *Bonner biblische Beiträge* 1 (1950), pp. 224–45.

"Die jüdischen und judenchristlichen Sekten im Lichte des

Handschriftenfundes von 'En Fešha" *Zeitschrift für katholische Theologie* 74 (1952), pp. 1–62.

"Die hebräischen Handschriften aus der Höhle von 'En Fešha", *Schweizer Rundschau* 52 (1952), pp. 89–95.

"Bemerkungen zum Verständnis einiger Termini in den Handschriften von 'En Fešha und im Damaskusdokument", *Theologische Literaturzeitung* 77 (1952), pp. 329–336.

"Der Sektenkanon von 'En Fešha und die Anfänge der jüdischen Gnosis", *Theologische Literaturzeitung* 78 (1953), pp. 495–506.

"Die Handschriftenfunde am Toten Meer", *Schweizerische Kirchenzeitung* 122 (1954), No. 3,4,5,6.

"Bergpredigt und Texte von 'En Fešha", *Tübinger theologische Quartalschrift* 135 (1955), pp. 320–37 (translated into English in Krister Stendahl, *The Scrolls and the New Testament*, New York, 1957; London, 1958; pp. 118–28).

"Die neuen Funde am Toten Meer und ihre Bedeutung für die Zeitgeschichte Jesu Christi", *Neues Abendland* 10 (1955), pp. 649–56.

"Zwei Messiasse aus dem Regelbuch von Chirbet Qumrân", *Judaica* 11 (1955), pp. 216–235.

"Der alttestamentliche Hintergrund der Vorstellung von den beiden Messiassen im Schrifttum von Chirbet Qumrân", *Judaica* 12 (1956) pp. 24–8.

"War Jesus sein Essener?" *Wort und Wahrheit* 11 (1956), pp. 687–97.

"Die ersten beiden Kolumnen der Kriegsrolle von Chirbet Qumrân", *Festschrift für Prof. Viktor Christian*, Vienna, 1956, pp. 93–9.

"Testament Juda 24 im Lichte der Texte von Chirbet Qumrân", *Wiener Zeitschrift für die Kunde des Morgenlandes* 53 (1957), pp. 227–36.

"Die Messiaslehre in den Texten von Chirbet Qumrân", *Biblische Zeitschrift* 1 (1957), pp. 177–97.

"Die religionsgeschichtliche Bedeutung der Handschriftenfunde vom Toten Meer", *Schweizerische Kirchenzeitung* 126 (1958) No. 10,11.

"Die Schriftrollen vom Toten Meer", *Münchener Theologische Zeitschrift* 9 (1958), pp. 142–8.

INDEX OF REFERENCES

(a) Biblical

(d) Qumrân Writings

(not included above)

(e) ANCIENT AUTHORS

(f) TALMUD AND MIDRASH